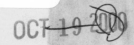

BENJAMIN BALTZLY

BENJAMIN BALTZLY

Photographs & Journal of an Expedition through British Columbia: 1871

Andrew Birrell

CHAMPLAIN COLLEGE

THE COACH HOUSE PRESS, TORONTO

For My Parents

Contents

Acknowledgments

All books are the result of the work and help of many people and this one is no exception. Without the kind permission of *The Gazette* of Montreal to reprint Baltzly's account of this trip there would, of course, have been no book.

I am grateful to Dr. W.I. Smith and the senior management of the Public Archives of Canada both for permission to use notes prepared for the exhibition 'Into the Silent Land' and for allowing the use of the Baltzly photographs in the National Photography Collection. The selection of Baltzly's work would have been far less interesting without the great cooperation of Stan Triggs of the Notman Photo Archives at McCord Museum. From Stan came not only help with the photographs, but also valuable information about Baltzly's work with the Notman studio. Margaret van Every and the Ontario Archives must be thanked for making access so easy to their excellent Baltzly photographs. James Borcoman and Ann Thomas of the National Gallery of Canada were extremely helpful with my last minute requests.

My colleagues in the National Photography Collection have offered continued encouragement and Richard Huyda and Lilly Koltun, in particular, gave me advice and criticism which I found valuable and for which I thank them. Reading manuscripts, I know, is not an exciting task. Joy Williams aided me considerably in the often thankless task of research.

Working with Stan Bevington and the staff of Coach House Press has been a pleasant experience. Were it not for Stan's gentle but frequent proddings I doubt that this book would have progressed this far.

Finally, I must give thanks to my wife, Betsy, who has been a constant help and encouragement in this and all my projects.

Part I
Introduction

Origins

1　James Richardson (1810-1883) joined the Geological Survey of Canada in 1846 and remained with it until 1883. He appears to have been the first of its employees to have used the camera, in conjunction with a survey of Labrador in 1862. Too few of the results have survived to able to judge his success. No report of this survey was printed.

2　John Hammond (1843-1939) was one of many artists who worked for the Notman Studio. He had a distinguished career as an artist in later years and attained recognition for a series of paintings of Western Canada commissioned by William Van Horne.

3　Quoted in A.R.C. Selwyn, 'Journal and Report of Preliminary Explorations in British Columbia,' in Geological Survey of Canada, *Report of Progress for 1871-72,* (Montreal: Dawson Bros., 1872), 17.

In 1871 the young confederation of Canada took a daring step forward when British Columbia was convinced to join the eastern provinces. There was a price though – the completion of a transcontinental railway to the new province within ten years, with construction starting in two. The government of Sir John A. Macdonald immediately appointed Sandford Fleming as Chief Engineer of the new project and Fleming quickly dispatched ten surveying parties to determine the best route for the railway to follow west from Ontario to the Pacific coast. The greatest attention was focused on British Columbia where the maze of mountains and jungle-like forests posed the most difficult problem.

Joseph Trutch, one of the negotiators for British Columbia, had urged that the railway survey be accompanied by a geological survey which would provide both general knowledge about the interior and specific information about the mineral wealth to be found along the proposed routes. Accordingly, plans were made by Alfred R.C. Selwyn, Director of the Geological Survey of Canada, for a small party to go to British Columbia in the 1871 season. Joseph Howe, Secretary of State for the Provinces, instructed Selwyn to learn as much as possible about the general geological features of the province and of the minerals to be found along the proposed routes.

The party sent by the Geological Survey consisted only of Selwyn and James Richardson, an experienced employee of long standing.[1] Accompanying them were two employees of the Montreal photographer William Notman, Benjamin F. Baltzly and John Hammond.[2] As late as June 6 Baltzly and Hammond had not been included in the survey proposal. It is unclear whether Selwyn or Notman was responsible for the idea, but Selwyn certainly favoured it for he had arranged with Sandford Fleming to share the travelling expenses of the photographers. Selwyn probably first broached the subject with Howe in a now missing letter of June 10. At any rate, in Howe's final authorization of the survey he granted Selwyn permission to take one of Notman's photographers along in order 'to secure accurate illustrations of the physical features of the country and of other objects of interest which may be met with during the exploration'.[3] Notman agreed to supply the equipment and to pay Baltzly and Hammond; in return he retained the negatives and all rights to them.

Benjamin Baltzly was born in Tuscarawas County, Ohio, on April 5, 1835, the seventh of eight children of John and Elizabeth Baltzly who were farmers in Sugar Creek Township. Nothing is known of his early adulthood or photo-

11

graphic experience except that he apparently passed the first thirty years of his life in Ohio.[4] When he arrived in Montreal sometime between July, 1866, and June, 1867, he was an experienced photographer.[5] He worked in the Montreal studio of J.G. Parks before opening his own studio at 372 Notre Dame Street during the first part of 1868.[6] However, Montreal at that time was a difficult place for a new photographer. In addition to the dominant firm of William Notman, the studios of James Inglis, J.G. Parks and Alexander Henderson had established reputations, while a host of smaller operators clustered at their heels.

Within a few months of opening his studio, Baltzly proposed publishing a paper entitled *The Photographer* with a free distribution of ten thousand.[7] There was no further mention of this publication and if it ever saw the light of day, no copies have survived. Moreover, Baltzly's ability to finance such a paper on a gratuitous basis is highly suspect.

In his spare time Baltzly was involved with the Working Women's Benefit and Employment Society of which he was a founder and the first President in 1869. His religious beliefs may have influenced his participation in the Society while the women he hired for his studio probably made him aware of the difficulties faced by self-supporting single women. The Society attempted to provide sick benefits and aided members in obtaining good positions, but although it was very active during 1869 it seems to have died shortly thereafter.[8]

Baltzly's name came to the fore again late in 1869 when he gave several stereopticon shows.[9] He remained in business, evidently in a small way, until April 24, 1870, when a fire swept through his studio destroying it.[10] A few weeks afterwards he began working for William Notman. Apart from this, little else is known of his life prior to the trip to British Columbia.

When Baltzly commenced his work with Notman he was probably involved primarily with portraiture. However he must have been an experienced view photographer and it is reasonable to assume that Notman considered him one of his most able employees since he entrusted the demanding and expensive work of the British Columbia trip to him.

4 *The Cambridge Chronicle*, July 14, 1883, 5, col. 3.

5 He later advertised that he had won three first prizes in exhibitions in 1863 and 1864 although he never stated where he had won these honours.

6 *The Witness* (Montreal), June 30, 1868, 2, col. 6.

7 Ibid., July 23, 1868, 3, col. 4.

8 Ibid., Mar. 11, 1869, 3, col. 1.

9 Ibid., Oct. 1, 1869, 2, col. 1; Dec. 1, 2, col. 1.

10 Ibid., April 25, 1870, 2, col. 2; *The Gazette* (Montreal), April 25, 1870, 2, col. 5-6.

The Trip to

British Columbia

From the outset both the Geological and the CPR survey teams were beset by difficulties. Selwyn's team had been late leaving Montreal and had experienced further delays at San Francisco and Victoria.[11] They reached Yale late in July only to find that all means of transportation had been hired by others. Consequently they were forced to continue on foot in temperatures which exceeded 100 degrees F. with the help of only a few Indian packers. They finally obtained transport at Lytton and, by means of wagon, foot and canoe, the whole party reached Kamloops on August 9. Once again they experienced difficulty in securing pack animals and handlers; as a result they did not begin the survey proper until August 18, at least a month later than desirable.

During all these delays Baltzly had been active taking almost fifty views along the route from Victoria to Kamloops, many of them at Selwyn's request, but many others for purely scenic or commercial interest. A number of these occasions are mentioned by both Baltzly and Selwyn.[12]

Selwyn had not decided which route he should examine until he reached Victoria. After discussion with Walter Moberly and Roderick McLennan he chose to follow McLennan's party which was to begin at Kamloops and ascend the North Thompson River, cross to Tête Jaune Cache and from there proceed through the Leather Pass, as the Yellowhead was then called, as far as Jasper House. He hoped to return via the Cariboo along a route that was to be explored by James A. Mahood. The route out was the reverse of that followed by Viscount Milton and Walter Butler Cheadle when they made their overland journey from east to west in 1861-62. In fact Selwyn's party carried a copy of Milton and Cheadle's *The North West Passage by Land* as a guide. Both Selwyn and Baltzly quoted from it frequently in their journals.

In spite of Milton and Cheadle's warnings to the contrary, Selwyn did not expect a trying journey, partly because McLennan and his men had preceded them and were cutting a trail. By the end of August they had reached Raft River and caught up with McLennan. From this point forward, says Selwyn, 'obstructions and difficulties of all kinds increased rapidly.' The first serious setback occurred at the impassable Murchison's Rapids about eight miles upstream from Mad River. Faced with seemingly impenetrable forest, no apparent trail, obstructive bluffs and lack of pasture for the horses, McLennan and Selwyn accepted the advice of their native guides and decided to follow an Indian trail which ascended Mad River, crossed the watershed of the mountains and descended to the Thompson again by the Blue River. Unfortunately the

11 Selwyn, 'Journal and Report,' 18-20.
12 Ibid., 23, 25.

13

trail was nowhere to be found and they were forced to cut their way through thick timber and swampy land. Progress slowed to a crawl and it was twelve days before they finally reached the Thompson again, on September 12. But here they found themselves in a thick cedar forest alternating with boggy creeks. During the next week they were able to cut only four and a half miles of trail. Baltzly quoted Milton and Cheadle with approval for they had commented of the same place that the trees were

prostrate, reclining, horizontal, propped up at different angles, timber of every size, in every state of growth and decay, in every possible condition, entangled in every possible combination.

At this juncture Selwyn realized that they would have to abandon their hope of reaching Jasper House. The survey was further jeopardized by the dangerously low level of their provisions. Selwyn had ordered enough for two months, thinking that would be adequate, but after five weeks they were nowhere near their target. Baltzly was made commissary and he immediately reduced daily rations by a quarter. Though this was trouble enough, the weather now turned against them. 'Rain, *rain*, RAIN, almost day and night, with but very few excepted days,' wrote Baltzly, while Selwyn almost daily recorded rainstorms in his journal. Frosts were now common at night and snow was beginning to appear on the mountainsides.

Throughout these difficulties, however, neither Baltzly nor Selwyn lost his ability to admire the beauty of the country. Baltzly, in particular, was aware of the picturesque nature of the scenery and on many occasions he gave extended descriptions of the country. He took numerous photographs often after considerable difficulty in reaching a vantage point; sometimes, after all the work, he decided the picture was not worth taking. At Wild Goose Camp near the Blue River he travelled 'half a mile through the worst wood I ever saw ... I at one time was tempted to return to camp. However, I persevered, and although I did not find the view of the falls worthy of a photograph, yet I was not sorry for having made the trip.'

Although Baltzly found the forests beautiful, he felt he was in an alien world since the sun never shone directly on the forest floor. Even when a strong wind bent the treetops, all remained perfectly still below. 'I at times,' he wrote, 'compared myself to a merman, who while at the bottom of the ocean, amid a large growth of queer seaweed ... should look up from his abo[d]e of peace, and see the surface of the water f[a]r above him, raging in a terrible storm.' It was at this time that he took the memorable photograph 'Forest Scene on the North Thompson 165 Miles above Kamloop'. [plate 45]

By October 13 the party had reached the Canoe River and was faced with the crucial decision of whether to press on or to turn back. The horses were extremely weak and the difficult crossing from the Mad River to the Blue was reported to be under eight inches of snow and nearly impassable. Selwyn, however, was still anxious to reach as far as the Yellowhead Pass so, on the advice of the Indian guide, Whooit Pask, he decided to make a flying visit through the Yellowhead Pass to Cowdung [Yellowhead] Lake, accompanied by Baltzly, Hammond, the guide and two packers. Baltzly packed his stereo equipment with misgivings. 'I felt rather averse to this undertaking,' he said, 'and could not enter into it as enthusiastically as some others, the reason being the lateness of the season, the jaded appearance of the horses, and the almost certainty of being snow-bound on our return to Kamloop.' After five days, almost all in the rain and on half rations, Selwyn decided to abandon the attempt and return to the camp at Canoe River. Like Moses and the Promised Land, wrote Baltzly, they were allowed to see their goal but not to enter it. 'Photographically speaking,' he complained 'it was a frantic leap after the shadow and losing the substance.'

My evil forebodings before we started were unfortunately realized. We lost the opportunity of taking views here at Canoe River which with a few exceptions, are as good as those we saw above, and the best of which I was not able to take on account of rain and continuous travel.

The return journey to Kamloops was also marred by difficulties. Abandoning the pack animals on October 28 at the forks of the North Thompson, they stopped for several days to repair a faulty cache. They then built several canoes and paddled their way rapidly down the North Thompson, constantly in danger of being frozen in. The physical hardships of the return trip are vividly recalled by Baltzly who suffered frostbite. The most trying moment for the photographer occurred while they were running the treacherous Murchison's Rapids when the canoe containing all of his 8 x 10 negatives overturned. 'One can imagine my feelings about that time,' he wrote, but when they retrieved the canoe they found that by a freak of luck the box containing the negatives had wedged under the crosspiece. After drying they were in perfect condition.

While portaging another of these rapids the group lost its largest canoe. As a result everything not essential, including the photographic equipment, had to be cached near Mad River.

The party finally arrived back in Kamloops on November 18, battling ice all the way. Of the hundred and fifty pack animals which had accompanied the parties of Selwyn and McLennan, only twenty-six returned to Kamloops; the rest perished. Yet in spite of all the trials they had experienced, Baltzly took an optimistic view of his experience:

... the first part of the journey was most delightful, but the last part was the extreme of *delightless*, except what pleasure we could get in '*roughing it*,' which was not a little.

The Photographs

Baltzly proved that he was a skilled photographer particularly when working with the 8 inch by 10 inch format, and his work is easily the best done in British Columbia during the decade. Even his straight scientific photographs have a strength in them that was never approached by the geologists themselves when they began carrying cameras a few years later.

It was a little unusual for a photographer to have accompanied the Geological Survey party, because under Sir William Logan, the former director, the Survey had refused to make use of the camera in the field. Logan had a practical reason for his attitude. He had experimented in the past and found that the bulky equipment required by the wet collodion process slowed the progress of surveys when they were in the field. The benefits obtained from accurate illustrations were, in his opinion, outweighed by the difficulties created.[13] Selwyn may have had an open mind on the subject, but he eventually accepted Logan's reasons.

Selwyn was obviously aware of the use made of the camera in explorations all over the world. In fact, when he had been director of the Geological Survey in Australia he had made use of the camera, though not with fully satisfactory results.[14] In 1869 Clarence King and Ferdinand Hayden had begun their now famous surveys of the American West and both had hired skilled photographers to accompany them to take views of the little known country and of interesting geological formations. Selwyn certainly knew of King's survey and may, therefore, have been familiar with the photographs taken by Timothy O'Sullivan. Certainly the frame of reference for Baltzly was the same as that for O'Sullivan and the photographers who followed him. So, although the reasons for Selwyn's decision to hire a photographer are still obscure, he was probably influenced by a general awareness of the medium's growing usefulness around the world in work similar to his.

No doubt the fact that William Notman supplied the photographers and their equipment and paid their salaries was a factor greatly favouring their inclusion on the survey. Nor is it surprising that Notman was involved. Doubtless he hoped to capitalize on the public interest in the province and on the possibilities offered by the mountainous country for new and exciting scenery. British Columbia was still remembered as the land of gold which had attracted tens of thousands from around the world only a decade previously. Both general public interest in the new province and the continuing public desire for views of the 'novel and peculiar', as Baltzly put it, made the investment a reasonable one. Undoubtedly Notman hoped to fill an anticipated public demand, and possibly

13   Public Archives of Canada, RG 45, vol. 74, Geological Survey of Canada Letterbooks, William Logan to E. J. Russell, June 11, 1868.

14   Ibid., vol. 76, A.R.C. Selwyn to B. Baltzly, Feb. 28, 1873.

a substantial government demand as well.

In spite of the official purpose of the photographs, the arrangements indicate that Baltzly really was to serve two masters and two purposes. The fact that so few photographs from the expedition have survived outside the official government agencies for which they were taken is an indication that Notman's investment was not rewarded. Baltzly himself announced that he was dissatisfied with the photographs, blaming the lack of success on their late start, the great difficulties of travelling and the unrelenting bad weather. Selwyn, on the other hand, appeared quite happy with the photographs which he characterized in his report to Joseph Howe as being 'very beautiful and interesting'. He made specific reference to over forty of them in order to illustrate various aspects of the geology he discussed.

Although Selwyn was satisfied with the results of Baltzly's work, he was dismayed at the cost of acquiring them. The total cost for the transportation of the two photographers was over three thousand dollars, nearly half of the cost of the entire geological expedition. And that, of course, did not include their salaries and equipment. Little wonder, then, that when Baltzly proposed setting up a photographic department for the Survey, Selwyn's response was negative:

It would doubtless be ... useful ... but I have grave doubts as regards its success in a financial point of view. It has already been tried here under Sir W.E. Logan's direction and was found not to work satisfactorily ... and my experience ... agrees with that of Sir William Logan ...[15]

It was the wet collodion process which lay at the heart of the problem. Because the glass plate had to be coated with collodion, then exposed and developed while the emulsion was still moist, an inordinate amount of fragile equipment had to be transported. In addition to Baltzly's 8 by 10 and stereo cameras, which were heavy in themselves, a complete darkroom had to be included: a portable darktent on a tripod, collodion, silver nitrate and baths, developer, fixer, clean water and glass plates, all in sufficient quantities to make more than the hundred and twenty negatives that were produced. All of this required at least one pack animal for transport, and a lengthy stop any time a photograph was taken. As Baltzly's account reveals, these preparations resulted in even greater difficulties once the group was in the mountains and forests.

When Selwyn wrote to Sandford Fleming explaining the costs involved in the photographic work he said, 'The great weight of the photographic apparatus

15 Op. cit.

(nearly 500 lbs.) has made the cost of the photographic branch of the expedition proportionately larger than that for geological purposes.'[16] His experience was not unique and the difficulties were as much due to the terrain of British Columbia as to the weight of the equipment. Ten years earlier the American section of the joint Boundary Commission which marked the 49th Parallel between British Columbia and Washington Territory abandoned its attempt to take photographs because of the difficulty of carrying the equipment through the dense forests. Lieutenant-Colonel John Hawkins who commanded the British section of the same survey was so deterred by his own experience in obtaining photographs that he recommended against the use of photography on similar expeditions in the future. In contrast, the American photographers working with the government surveys in the West in the 1870s seem not to have suffered such severe problems, neither is there a hint of difficulty on the North American Boundary Commission working across the Prairies from 1872 to 1875. It would seem, therefore, that the greatest source of difficulty lay in the mountainous and heavily forested country of British Columbia.

Even a cursory perusal of Baltzly's and Selwyn's accounts of the journey will impress the reader with the difficulties they had to overcome. That any photographs at all were taken in the interior is a cause for wonder, and that so many were taken and brought back is astonishing. Fate alone is to be thanked, for on more than one occasion the whole season's work was in danger of destruction.

An examination of the photographs reveals that the majority of them were taken for geological purposes. Many which at first glance appear to have served commercial ends also illustrated the geology of the land. Others, both in subject matter and title, had an obviously scientific purpose. It is to be expected that the least commercial photographs would be those taken in the wilderness, yet even photographs taken for strictly personal reasons by Baltzly were used by Selwyn and were probably taken with his approval if not at his instigation. Selwyn specifically refers to 'Forest Scene on the North Thompson' [plate 45] in his report, while his interest in the Garnet River area is evident from the fact that he made a sketch of the river below their camp and actually visited the falls to examine the geological structure in the vicinity.[17] Baltzly's account reveals that the former photograph was taken to show the density of the forest and the consequent difficulty of cutting a trail. But his description of the Garnet River Cascade [plates 48 and 49], which is quite apart from Selwyn's interest in it, is pure Romanticism; it is evident that he was deeply moved by the scenery. On a

16 Op. cit., A.R.C. Selwyn to Sandford Fleming, March 30, 1872.
17 Selwyn, 'Journal and Report,' 35.

number of occasions he broke into rapturous descriptions of the beauty he saw and usually his thoughts were drawn from his surroundings to the grandeur of God.

Although Selwyn speaks quite clearly of Baltzly's having taken one hundred and twenty negatives, thirty-six 8x10 and eighty-four stereo, Notman's studio index records one hundred and twenty-five (see Checklist). Selwyn stated in his report to Joseph Howe that he was enclosing a full set of photographs. However, no full set now exists even when all the extant collections are joined. In addition to the set sent to Howe, the Geological Survey of Canada retained at least thirty-three of the large format prints and a further twenty-six were purchased by Sandford Fleming. It is not known if they originally purchased sets of the stereos as well.

There remain a few points about the extant prints which are worth mentioning. Those purchased by Sandford Fleming were straight prints from the original negatives with no identifying information on their face. Later, as many of the plates reveal, many of the negatives were renumbered by Notman for inclusion in his view series. These have a title, often vague and sometimes completely wrong, in the lower right corner. Prints from the 8x10 negatives made after the renumbering frequently have clouds printed in from a separate negative. This was a common practice at the time, necessary because the emulsion was more sensitive to the blue end of the spectrum. Consequently when exposures were made for a landscape the sky was well overexposed and printed as a blank white. Apparently Notman had a very small repertoire of cloud negatives at this time, for only two appear in the photographs – time and again. For instance, the first two of the four part panorama of Victoria Harbour [plates 3 and 4] have exactly the same cloud formation, all the more identifiable because of a flaw in the negative. The clouds were often sloppily arranged so that they merged with the ground [plate 19]. Clouds were printed in sometimes in an attempt to capture the haziness of the distance which was termed aerial perspective. This was deemed to be a virtue in landscape photography. A comparison of plate 54 and plate 55 reveals how unwanted detail in the distant mountains was suppressed by careful printing and the addition of a cloud negative even though the cloud effect is not convincing.

A strange anomaly appears in the photograph from Sandford Fleming's collection which is printed as plate 40. A combination of the foreground of plate 39 and the mountainous backdrop of plate 38, this may be an attempt by the studio to salvage a reasonable print from two relatively poor negatives. Plate 38 seems to have been exposed for the mountains, thus leaving the foreground badly underexposed. Certainly the combination print would have been useless as geological evidence for Selwyn.

Whatever were Notman's and Selwyn's reactions to the results of Baltzly's work, we must assert today that the body of photographs he produced was a notable accomplishment, not only for the evidence it provides of the history of a river now conquered by the railway, but also for the technical and, occasionally, for the artistic excellence of the results.

Later Career

Much less is known of Baltzly's subsequent career and work. He apparently enjoyed his work with the Geological Survey and, perhaps chafing at working for Notman, he proposed establishing a permanent photographic unit there. The only account of his life states that he travelled frequently for Notman and had gone to Harvard University in 1873 to photograph several classes.[18] He acquired a good reputation for his photographs of large groups and took many class pictures for a number of Ivy League colleges. Although it is impossible to pinpoint which photographs Baltzly took, it is probable that many of the prints to be found at Harvard and other colleges bearing the names of Notman and Pach Brothers were taken by him.

Baltzly was on the staff of Notman's Montreal studio from May, 1870, to July, 1875, and again from May, 1876, to August, 1877. He dropped from sight and reappeared in Cambridge, Massachusetts, as manager of the Pach Brothers studio beginning probably sometime early in 1879. In December of 1882 he purchased the studio of George K. Warren in Cambridge and was warmly commended for his work in *The Cambridge Chronicle*. On July 10, 1883, only six months later, he died from the effects of acute gastritis.

At his death he was conducting a successful business and had become well-known for the quality of his large group portraits. No mention is made of any activity in the landscape field and there are no outdoor photographs from the post-1871 period that can be attributed to him with certainty. Baltzly's professional life was spent in relative obscurity and even those photographs for which he is now celebrated seem to have gained him only the slightest recognition at the time he took them. Like so many other men who played a small part in the explorations for and the construction of the Canadian Pacific Railway, he viewed his work as a job to be done well and he asked little beyond the remuneration he received for doing it.

18 *The Cambridge Chronicle*, July 14, 1883, 5, col. 4.

The Journal

The text of Baltzly's account originally appeared in *The Gazette* of Montreal during the summer of 1872. The text is given here without change, but wherever geographical names have changed I have indicated the modern name in a footnote. Unfortunately, it has not been possible to identify modern names for all the places Baltzly mentions.

Apparently Baltzly kept a diary of his trip and the bulk of his account follows the diary verbatim. However, in preparing it for publication he made additions and clarifications. Hence the reader will find a sometimes confusing shift from present to past tense. Baltzly appears to be reliable in his details and, except for a few minor points which are indicated in the text, he and Selwyn are in agreement in their accounts.

Bibliography

Newspapers
1. *The Cambridge Chronicle*, 1879-1882
2. *The Gazette* (Montreal), 1867-1870
3. *The Witness* (Montreal), 1867-1870

Manuscript and Other
1. Public Archives of Canada, RG 45, Geological Survey of Canada Letterbooks.
2. A.R.C. Selwyn, 'Journal and Report of Preliminary Explorations in British Columbia,' in Geological Survey of Canada, *Report of Progress for 1871-72*. Montreal: Dawson Bros., 1872.

Photographs
I have been able to find four collections of Baltzly photographs, none of them complete, and all of them attributed to Notman.

The largest collection is to be found in the Notman Photographic Archives, McCord Museum, Montreal. In addition to the prints, Notman Photo Archives also has some of the original 8x10 glass plate negatives. Unfortunately the stereo negatives were lost or destroyed sometime in the distant past.

The National Photography Collection of the Public Archives of Canada, Ottawa, has almost all of the 8x10 prints, some of them in duplicate form. They are found in the Sandford Fleming Collection and in the Geological Survey of Canada Collection. The prints from the latter appear to have been printed at a later date, but how much later it is impossible to say. They differ in having printed titles on the photograph and in some cases clouds have been printed in.

The Ontario Archives, Toronto, has approximately twenty views in the Rathbun Album, a mixture of 8x10 and stereo formats. The prints are in excellent condition.

A further twenty-six prints are to be found in the Kamloops Museum in British Columbia, but I was unable to examine these in person.

Part II
A Portfolio of Photographs by Benjamin Baltzly

Checklist of
B.F. Baltzly
Photographs

plate 1	69901	Victoria Harbour from St. Nicholas Hotel, July 17-25. PAC (C-21397)
	69902	Victoria Harbour from St. Nicholas Hotel, July 17-25. NGC
plate 2	69903	Government Street, Victoria, July 17-25.
plate 3	69904	Victoria from Mission Hill, July 17-25. PAC (PA-22610)
plate 4	69905	Victoria from Mission Hill, July 17-25. PAC
plate 5	69906	Victoria from Mission Hill, July 17-25. PAC (C-21400)
plate 6	69907	Victoria from Mission Hill, July 17-25. PAC (C-21399)
	69908	Victoria from Mission Hill, July 17-25.
	69909	Victoria from Mission Hill, July 17-25.
plate 7	69910	Ice grooved rocks at Finlayson's Point, Victoria, July 17-25. NPA
	69911	Ice grooved rocks at Finlayson's Point, Victoria, July 17-25.
	69912	Ice grooved rocks at Finlayson's Point, Victoria, July 17-25.
	69913	The first Canadian Pacific R.R. and Geological Survey parties for British Columbia, July 22. Left to right; L.N. Rheaumis, Roderick McLennan, A.S. Hall, W.W. Ireland, Alfred Selwyn, Alex Maclennan, Walter Moberly, C.E. Gillette, James Richardson, – – McDonald, George Watt.
plate 8	69914	The first Canadian Pacific R.R. and Geological Survey parties for British Columbia, July 22. Left to right; L.N. Rheaumis, Roderick McLennan, A.S. Hall, W.W. Ireland, Alfred Selwyn, Alex Maclennan, Walter Moberly, C.E. Gillette, James Richardson, – – McDonald, George Watt. PAC (PA-22611)
plate 9	69915	On the Fraser River, 7½ miles from Yale, July 28. NPA
plate 10	69916	Halt for dinner on the Fraser River, July 28. NPA
plate 11	69917	Spuzzum River from Cariboo Road, July 28. PAC (PA-22603)
	69918	Spuzzum River from Cariboo Road, July 28. NPA
plate 12	69919	Alexandria Suspension Bridge over the Fraser River, July 28-29. NPA
plate 13	69920	East abutment of the Alexandria Suspension Bridge, July 28-29. NPA
plate 14	69921	Lytton, August 1. NPA
plate 15	69922	Ox team resting at Lytton, August 1. NPA
plate 16	69923	View on the Thompson River, 2 miles from Lytton, August 1-2. NPA
	69924	View on the Thompson River, 2 miles from Lytton, August 1-2.
plate 17	69925	View on the Thompson River, 3 miles from Lytton, August 1-2. NPA
plate 18	69926	Hell's Gate on the Thompson River, August 2-3. NPA
plate 19	69927	Indian encampment on the Thompson River, August 2-3. PAC (C-46347)
plate 20	69928	Indian encampment on the Thompson River, August 2-3. NPA
plate 21	69929	Teamsters breakfasting at Bonaparte, August 4. NPA
plate 22	69930	Teamsters preparing to move. Bonaparte, August 4. NPA
plate 23	69931	Savona Ferry, August 4-7. PAC (C-71205)
	69932	Savona Ferry, August 4-7.
plate 24	69933	Tranquille Mills, Kamloops Lake, August 9-12. PAC (C-23226)
	69934	Tranquille Mills, Kamloops Lake, August 9-12.
	69935	William Fortune and friends, August 9-12.
	69936	View east from Tranquille Mills, August 9-12.
	69937	View northwest from Tranquille Mills, August 9-12.
	69938	View west from Tranquille Mills giving a distant view of Battle Bluff, August 9-12.
plate 25	69939	Basaltic rocks at Battle Bluff, Kamloops Lake, August 9-12. PAC (PA-22613)
	69940	Basaltic rocks at Battle Bluff, Kamloops Lake, August 9-12.

plate 44	69973	Glaciers on the north Thompson River, September 20-24. PAC (PA-22601)
plate 45	69974	Forest trees on the North Thompson River, 165 miles above Kamloops, September 20-24. PAC (PA-22606)
plate 46	69975	Geological Survey camp on the North Thompson, 165 miles above Kamloops. After a stormy night, September 20-24. NPA
plate 47	69976	Mount Cheadle on the North Thompson River showing the upper part of Garnet River, September 29. PAC
plate 48	69977	Cascade on the Garnet River, September 29. PAC (C-71204)
plate 49	69978	Cascade on the Garnet River, September 29.
	69979	Cascade on the Garnet River, September 29. PAC (PA-22607)
	69980	Cascade on the Garnet River, September 29.
	69981	Cascade on the Garnet River, September 29.
	69982	Mountain scenery from the Forks of the North Thompson River, October 6.
	69983	Mountain scenery from the Forks of the North Thompson River, October 6.
plate 50	69984	Snow-clad mountains on the North Branch of the North Thompson River, October 6. NPA
plate 51	69985	Snow-clad mountains on the North Branch of the North Thompson River, October 6. PAC
plate 52	69986	Beaver Creek on the North Branch of the North Thompson River, October 7. NPA
plate 53	69987	Fallen timber on the North Branch of the North Thompson River, October 9. PAC (PA-22609)
plate 54 and 55	69988	Mount Milton on the North Thompson River, October 11. PAC
plate 56	69989	Milton Range from Albreda Lake, October 11-12. NPA
plate 57	69990	Mountain scenery near Albreda Lake, October 11-12. NPA
	69991	Albreda Lake valley, October 11-12.
plate 58	69992	The photographer of the Geological Survey in camp near Albreda Lake, October 12. NPA
plate 59	69993	Geological Survey party in camp at Canoe River, October 14. Alfred Selwyn at centre with John Hammond (left centre) and Benjamin Baltzly (right centre). PAC (PA-22612)
plate 60	69994	Northwest view from the lower end of Moose Lake, October 19. NPA
plate 61	69995	West from lower end of Moose Lake, October 19. NPA
	69996	South from lower end of Moose Lake, October 19. NPA
plate 62	69997	Moose Lake, October 19.
	69998	Mountain scenery near the Grand Forks of the Fraser River, October 23.
	69999	Mountain scenery near the Grand Forks of the Fraser River, October 23.
	70000	Mountain scenery near the Grand Forks of the Fraser River, October 23.
	70001	Mountain scenery at Selwyn River near Cranberry Lake, October 24.
	70002	Mountain scenery at Selwyn River near Cranberry Lake, October 24.
	70003	Mountain scenery at Selwyn River near Cranberry Lake, October 24.
	70004	View from Selwyn River near Cranberry Lake, looking toward Tête Jaune Cache, October 24.
	70005	Mount Thompson on Canoe River near Cranberry Lake, October 24.
	70006	Confluence of the McLennan and Canoe River valleys, October 24.
	70007	Canoe River valley, October 24.
	70008	Canoe River Gap, October 24.
plate 63	70009	Cranberry Lake, October 24. NPA
	70010	Cranberry Lake and Tête Jaune Cache, October 24.

plate 64	70011	Caching provisions at the Forks of the North Thompson River, October 30. PAC (PA-22605)
plate 65	70012	Geological and c.p.r.r. Survey caching provisions at the Forks of the North Thompson River, October 30. NPA
	70013	Geological and c.p.r.r. Survey caching provisions at the Forks of the North Thompson River, October 30.
plate 66	70014	View at Upper Gate of Murchison's Rapids on the North Thompson River, November 6-7. PAC (PA-22608)
	70015	View at Upper Gate of Murchison's Rapids on the North Thompson River, November 6-7.
	70016	View at Upper Gate of Murchison's Rapids on the North Thompson River, November 6-7.
plate 67	70017	View at the Lower End of the Upper Gate of Murchison's Rapids on the North Thompson River, November 6-7. PAC (PA-22617)
	70018	View at the Lower End of the Upper Gate of Murchison's Rapids on the North Thompson River, November 6-7.
	70019	View at the Lower End of the Upper Gate of Murchison's Rapids on the North Thompson River, November 6-7.
plate 68	70020	Portaging canoes at Upper Gate of Murchison's Rapids, November 6-7. PAC (PA-22618)
plate 69	70021	General view at the mouth of the Lower Gate of Murchison's Rapids on the North Thompson River, November 7-8. PAC (PA-22614)
	70022	General view at the mouth of the Lower Gate of Murchison's Rapids on the North Thompson River, November 7-8.
	70023	General view at the mouth of the Lower Gate of Murchison's Rapids on the North Thompson River, November 7-8.
plate 70	70024	Photographer's tent at the Lower Gate of Murchison's Rapids, November 8-9. Benjamin Baltzly (standing) and John Hammond. PAC (PA-22604)
plate 71	70025	Lower Gate of Murchison's Rapids on the North Thompson River, November 8-9. NPA

The titles found in the checklist represent a compilation of several sources, some of them in conflict. The least reliable source is the titles appearing on the face of some of the photographs. In some cases they were completely wrong. The dates are almost always deduced from a comparison with Baltzly's account and because of this they may occasionally be out by a few days.

Abbreviations
PAC National Photography Collection, Public Archives of Canada, Ottawa.
NGC National Gallery of Canada, Ottawa.
NPA Notman Photographic Archives, McCord Museum, Montreal.

The numbers appearing after PAC (eg. C-21397) are copy negative numbers which should be quoted when requesting copies of the photographs.

The Plates

1   Victoria from St. Nicholas Hotel, July 17-25. PAC

2 Government Street, Victoria, July 17-25. NGC

3 Victoria from Mission Hill, July 17-25 (Panorama 1). PAC

4 Victoria from Mission Hill, July 17-25 (Panorama 2). PAC

5 Victoria from Mission Hill, July 17-25 (Panorama 3). PAC

632—VICTORIA, B. C. FROM MISSION HILL

6 Victoria from Mission Hill, July 17-25 (Panorama 4). PAC

7 Ice grooved rocks at Finlayson's Point, Victoria, July 17-25. NPA

8 The first Canadian Pacific R.R. and Geological Survey parties for British Columbia, July 22. Left to right: L.N. Rheaumis, Roderick McLennan, A.S. Hall, W.W. Ireland, Alfred Selwyn, Alex Maclennan, Walter Moberly, C.E. Gillette, James Richardson, – – McDonald, George Watt. PAC

9 On the Fraser River [probably 69915]. NPA

10 On the Fraser River [probably 69916]. NPA

11 Spuzzum River from Cariboo Road, July 28. PAC

12 Alexandria Suspension Bridge over the Fraser River, July 28-29. NPA

673—SUSPENSION BRIDGE ACROSS THE FRASER

13 East abutment of the Alexandria Suspension Bridge over the Fraser River, July 28-29. NPA

14 Lytton, August 1. NPA

15 Ox team resting at Lytton, August 1. NPA

653—ON THE NORTH THOMPSON RIVER, B. C.

16 View on the Thompson River, 2 miles from Lytton, August 1-2. NPA

17 View on the Thompson River, 3 miles from Lytton, August 1-2. NPA

654—HELLS GATE ON THE THOMPSON RIVER B

18 Hell's Gate on the Thompson River, August 2-3. NPA

19 Indian encampment on the Thompson River, August 2-3. PAC

20 Indian encampment on the Thompson River, August 2-3. NPA

21   Teamsters breakfasting at Bonaparte, August 4. NPA

22   Teamsters preparing to move. Bonaparte, August 4. NPA

23 Savona Ferry, August 4-7. PAC

24 Tranquille Mills, Kamloops Lake, August 9-12. PAC

25 Basaltic rocks at Battle Bluff, Kamloops Lake, August 9-12. PAC

26 Battle Bluff, Kamloops Lake, August 9-12. NPA

27 South side, Kamloops Lake, August 9-12. NPA

28 Gravel banks and columns, Tranquille River 3 miles from its mouth, August 9-12. PAC

29 Kamloops, August 13-19. NPA

30 Junction of the North and South Thompson Rivers at Kamloops, August 13-19. PAC

31 North Thompson River valley, August 13-19. NPA

659—INDIAN RESERVE ON THE THOMPSON B. C

32 Red Pine Indian Reserve on the North Thompson River, August 23. NPA

33 Assiniboine Bluff on the North Thompson River, August 24. PAC

34 Raft River Cascade near the junction with the North Thompson River, August 28. PAC

35 Mad River near its junction with the North Thompson River, September 1-4. PAC

730—GEO. SURVEY ENCAMPMENT, B.C

36 Geological Survey encampment [probably 69964]. NPA

37 Murchison Lake at head of Mad River, September 6-7. NPA

38 Selkirk Mountains as seen from the top of the mountain near the confluence of the Blue and North Thompson Rivers, September 9-11. PAC

39 Selkirk Mountains as seen from the top of the mountain near the confluence of the Blue and North Thompson Rivers, September 9-11. PAC

40 Selkirk Mountains as seen from the top of the mountain near the confluence of the Blue and North
Thompson Rivers, September 9-11. [Composite of plates 38 and 39]

41 Selkirk Mountains as seen from the top of the mountain near the confluence of the Blue and North Thompson Rivers, September 9-11. PAC

42 Lake on top of mountain [probably 69970]. NPA

43 Lake on top of mountain [probably 69972]. NPA

44 Glaciers on the North Thompson River, September 20-24. PAC

45 Forest trees on the North Thompson River, 165 miles above Kamloops, September 20-24. PAC

46 Camping on the Thompson River [probably 69975]. NPA

693—MOUNT CHEADLE, ON THE N. THOMPSON RIVER B.C

47 Mount Cheadle on the North Thompson River, showing the Garnet River Cascade, September 29. PAC

50 Snow-clad mountains on the North Branch of the North Thompson River, October 6. NPA

SIZE 63 IN.

693—MOUNT CHEADLE, ON THE N. THOMPSON RIVER B.C

47 Mount Cheadle on the North Thompson River, showing the Garnet River Cascade, September 29. PAC

48 Cascade on the Hammond [Garnet] River, September 29. PAC

49 Cascade on the Hammond [Garnet] River, September 29. PAC

50 Snow-clad mountains on the North Branch of the North Thompson River, October 6. NPA

51 Glaciers on the North Thompson River [probably 69985]. PAC

52 Beaver Creek on the North Branch of the North Thompson River, October 7. NPA

53 Fallen timber on the North Thompson River, October 9. PAC

54 Mount Milton on the North Thompson River, October 11. PAC

55 Mount Milton on the North Thompson River, October 11. NPA [modern print from the original negative].

56 Milton Range from Albreda Lake, October 11-12. NPA

57 Mountain scenery near Albreda Lake, October 11-12. NPA

58 The photographer of the Geological Survey in camp near Albreda Lake, October 12. NPA.

59 Geological Survey party in camp at Canoe River, October 14. Alfred Selwyn at centre with John Hammond (left centre) and Benjamin Baltzly (right centre). **PAC**

60 Moose Lake, October 19 [probably 69994]. NPA

61 Moose Lake, October 19 [probably 69995]. NPA

686—MOOSE LAKE, B.C.

62 Moose Lake, October 19 [probably 69997]. NPA

709—CRANBERRY LAKE, B.C.

63 Cranberry Lake, October 24. NPA

64 Caching provisions at the Forks of the North Thompson River, October 30. PAC

65 Geological and c.p.r.r. Survey caching provisions, etc., at the Forks of the North Thompson River, October 30. NPA

66 View at Upper Gate of Murchison's Rapids on the North Thompson River, November 6-7. PAC

67 View at the Lower End of the Upper Gate of Murchison's Rapids, in the North Thompson River, November 6-7. PAC

68 Portaging canoes at Upper Gate of Murchison's Rapids, November 6-7. PAC

69 General view at the mouth of the Lower Gate of Murchison's Rapids on the North Thompson River, November 7-8. PAC

70 Photographer's tent at the Lower Gate of Murchison's Rapids, November 8-9. Benjamin Baltzly (standing) and John Hammond. PAC

71 Lower Gate of Murchison's Rapids on the North Thompson River, November 8-9. NPA

Part III
The Journal of an Expedition through British Columbia: 1871

CHAPTER I

Seven Days in the Cars from the Atlantic to the Pacific

The Gazette, June 18, 1872

If on the evening of the 26th of June, 1871, you had been at the Bonaventure Depot, at Montreal, you would have seen, prominent in the throng, four men bidding adieu to their friends. Upon inquiry you would have been told that they were two Geologists, namely, Messrs. A.R.C. Selwyn, Director of the Geological Survey of Canada, and J. Richardson; one Photographer, B.F. Baltzly, from Mr. Wm. Notman's staff of operators; and his assistant, John Hammond, bound for the wilds of British Columbia on a geological and photographic expedition. Their course of travel lay from Montreal to San Francisco, via Detroit, Chicago, Omaha, and across the Union, and Central Pacific R.R.; from San Francisco by steamer to Victoria, Vancouver's Island; then again by steamer up the Strait of Juan de Feuca, through the Gulf of Georgia, up the Fraser River, past New Westminster, on to Yale, which is at the head of navigation, and from Yale to explore the interior as circumstances would permit.

As can be inferred from the above we left Montreal on the evening of the 26th of June, last [1871]. In two and a half days we were travelling through the beautiful prairie land of Illinois and Iowa. The country and cities along the Grand Trunk R.R. to Detroit are so well known that I shall leave that part of our journey unnoticed. We were all particularly attracted by the appearance of the country along the line of travel through Michigan, Illinois and Iowa. Much of the land is prairie, slightly undulating, thickly settled and well cultivated, except Western Iowa. For hundreds of miles nothing could be seen except corn, growing luxuriantly, interspersed with grain fields of every description, and beautiful homesteads. On the 31st of June we arrived at Omaha, a pretty, thriving little city on the west bank of the Missouri River. It claims 25,000 inhabitants. It is the eastern terminus of the great Trans-Continental R.R. Line. Soon after our arrival we entered the cars of the Union Pacific R.R., in which we travelled to Ogden, a distance of 1,032 miles without change of cars.

Passing through Nebraska, and part of Wyoming Territory, we arrived at Sherman, on the evening of the 30th of June, 549 miles west of Omaha. This is the highest point on the Trans-Continental, being 8,242 feet above the level of the sea. Now we begin to descend the western slope of the Black Ridge, across barren plains, between rocky ridges or cliffs of mountains. In the afternoon of the 1st of July we arrived at Wahsatch, 966 miles west of Omaha. Nine miles further on is Castle Rock. Between this place and Omaha there is not much of interest as far as scenery is concerned.

The general aspect of Nebraska Territory is rolling prairie. In the more eastern parts the soil seems to be very rich, and appears to be easily brought under cultivation. But the western part of it has rather poor soil. The face of Wyoming Territory is broken by high ranges of mountains. In the western part of the territory there are large tracts of prairie land of poor quality, much flecked with alkali, but in the eastern portion, the prairies are larger, more fertile, and covered with an abundant crop of grass.

Now and then emigrant trains were seen wending their way along the dusty plains toward the far west. Here and there in the plains of Nebraska the antelope, not pleased with the grating noise of the long trains, leaves its quiet grazing and hastes away on either side.

Now we pass some Red Men's camp. Anon we pass *Prairie Dog City,* with its myriads of quaint little inhabitants, who upon the approach of the train scamper off to their *houses.* Here they stop and perch themselves upon their hind legs, or feet, and await further developements, or bark at the train as it passes. Their cities frequently cover a space of from two to three miles square. The prairie dog is about the size of a guinea pig. It is of a light brown color upon the back, and white on the belly and on the inside of the legs. It appears to be very active in its habits, and graceful in appearance. Their dwelling consists of a little mound – with a hole in the top – from a foot to a foot and a-half high, raised by dirt excavated from their burrows. It is said that owls and rattlesnakes are their close companions, and in the majority of cases each burrow is occupied by a prairie dog, an owl, and a rattlesnake. It seems they do not quarrel, but are really a happy family.

The scenes from Castle Rock to Uintah, a distance of 51 miles, are grand beyond conception. In looking upon them I cannot avoid saying: How wonderful are all thy ways, O Lord, how full is the earth of thy marvelous works! After leaving Castle Rock we descended the Canyon amid some of the grandest and wildest scenery imaginable. We did not creep on it as though we mistrusted our powers, but with a snort and roar the engine plunged down the defile which momentarily increased to a gorge, and only became in a short distance a grand and awful chasm. About seven miles below Castle Rock, we beheld the natural bridge, a conglomerate formation, spanning a cleft in the wall on the right hand side. Further on is the Hanging Rock, which looks as though the elements have been wearing the centre of it away for centuries until they have succeeded in cutting it in two, save the harder crusts which now span the channel made by *father time.* The left hand side of the Canyon presents but few attractions compared to the bolder and loftier bluffs opposite. Its wall breaks away and recedes in sloping and grassy hill sides, while we know not what lies beyond these walls to our right, for they close the view in that direction. Wall, solid wall, broken wall, walls of sandstone, walls of granite, and walls mixed with clay rise far above us and shut from vision whatever lies beyond. The beauties of Echo Canyon are so many, so majestic, so awe inspiring in their sublimity that, in passing I was led to think of the greatness, majesty and glory of the Creator of all these wonders.

As we rush swiftly along, seemingly beneath those towering heights, I will attempt to note some of the most prominent features. The only difficulty is we hardly see them all as the cars thunder along, waking the echoes amid these castellated monuments of red rock, whose towering domes, and frowning buttresses gave the name to this remarkable opening of the Wahsatch Mountains. Four miles below Hanging Rock the walls rise in massive majesty – the prominent features of the Canyon. Rain, wind and time combined here to destroy them, but in vain. Centuries have come and gone since that mighty convulsion shook the earth to its center, when Echo and Weber Canyon sprang into existence, whose birth was heralded by throes such as the earth may never feel again; and still the mighty walls of this Echo remain, bidding defiance alike to time and his co-laborers, the elements; still hangs this delicate frill and frost work from the wall, still the pillar, column, dome and spires stand boldly forth in all their grand, wild and wierd beauty, to entrance the spectator and fill his mind with wonder and awe. Six miles below Hanging Rock, upon the topmost heights of the towering cliffs, a thousand feet above the bed of the Canyon, can be seen the fortifications erected by the Mormons to defend this pass against the army under Johnson, sent out in 1857 by Uncle

Sam. These fortifications consist of massive rocks, placed on the verge of the precipice, which were to be toppled over onto the heads of the soldiers below. But they had no occasion to try the experiment, so the rocks remain.

On goes the engine, whirling us past castle, cathedral, towering columns and rugged battlements; past ravines which cut the walls from crest to base in awful chasms, shooting over bridges, flying past and under the overhanging walls, when, after crossing the Echo Creek numerous times, we rush past the Witches' Cave and Pulpit Rock, our engine giving a loud scream of warning to the brakeman, who, throwing on the brakes, brings the train to a stop, and we are at Weber River and Echo City Station. This place is situated at the head of the bluff, which towers far above it.

Leaving this station the cars speed along the banks of Weber River for about six miles when they enter the Narrows of Weber Canyon, through which the road is cut for two miles, most of the way on the side of the steep mountain that drops its base in the river bed. The river for about 40 miles rushes foaming along between two massive mountain walls, which close the landscape on either side. Now the torrent plunges over some mighty rock which has fallen from the towering cliff; anon, it whirls around in frantic struggles to escape from the boiling eddy, thence springing forward over a short, smooth rapid, only to repeat the plunge again and again, until it breaks forth into the plains, whence it glides away toward the lake, as though exhausted with its wild journey through the canyon.

Shortly after leaving the Narrows we came to the thousand-mile tree — a thrifty branching pine — bearing on its trunk a sign board that tells the western-bound traveller that he has passed over 1,000 miles of railway from Omaha. Near this tree are two ridges of granite rock on the left-hand side of the road, reaching from the river nearly to the summit of a sloping grass-clad mountain. These are called the serrated rocks, or Devil's slides. They are from 50 to 200 feet high, narrow slabs, standing on edge, as though forced out of the mountainside. The two ridges run parallel with each other about 100 feet apart, the space between being covered with grass, wild flowers, and climbing vines. Rushing swiftly along we lose sight of these rocks to behold others more grand, of different shapes and massive proportions. The mountains seem to have been dove-tailed together, and then torn rudely asunder, leaving the rough promontories and rugged chasms as so many obstacles to bar our progress. Now we shoot across the river and dart through a tunnel 550 feet long, cut in solid rock, with heavy cuts and fills at either entrance. The frowning cliffs again bar our way, and again we cross the roaring torrent and burrow under the point of a rocky promontory. Here the road stretches across a pretty little valley — known as the Round Valley. Dashing along with but a moment to spare in which to note its beauties, the massive walls, with barely room for the track between them and the foaming torrents at our feet; on, around a jutting point, and again we emerge into a lengthened widening of the canyon and we pause for a moment at Weber station. Two miles further on we again enter towering mountains, the valley now lost in the narrow gloomy gorge, when suddenly we come to the Devil's Gate station, 12 miles from Weber. Soon after leaving the station the brink of the torrent is neared, and the wild scenery of the Devil's Gate is before us. Onward toils the long train across the bridge, 50 feet above the seething caldron of waters, where massive, frowning rocks rear their crests far up towards the black and threatening clouds which hover over this witch's caldron. With bated breath we gaze on this wild scene, and vainly try to analyze our feelings, in which awe, wonder, and admiration are blended. No time for thought as to how or when this mighty work was accomplished, no time or inclination to compare the works of nature with the puny work beneath us, but onward with quickening speed down the right bank of the stream; on between these massive piles, worn and seamed in their ceaseless struggles with the destroying hand of time; on to where yon opening of light marks the open country, on past towering mountains and topling rocks, until we catch a view of the broad, sunlit plains, and from the last and blackest of the buttresses which guard the entrance into Weber we emerge to light and beauty, to catch the first view of the Great Salt Lake, to behold broad plains, which stretch their lines of waving green and golden shades beyond. We have now passed through Wah-satch mountains, and are fairly in the Great Salt Lake Valley.

In due time we arrived at Ogden. This is the connecting link between the Union and Central Pacific Railway. After a few hours' delay we again took cars, in which we crossed the Central Pacific Railway to San Francisco, crossing the rich and fertile plains of Humbolt Valley; on through the Great Nevada Desert, covered, in some places thickly, in others sparsely, with sage brush, having neither wood nor water, and whose broad expanse is broken only by low rolling hills as bare and forbidding as the desert itself. As we hurry along over this un-hospitable waste as fast as we can, what was before a barren, cheerless waste is suddenly transformed into a beautiful landscape of waving trees, green meadows, and rushing streams by the Mirage. On through whirlwind plains, where nothing but sage brush, whirlwinds, dust and heat exists during this season of the year. (The thermometer reading 99° in the shade, yet strange to say the heat is not oppressive.) On the morning of the 8th of July we were on the top or summit of the Sierra Nevada. From this summit to Colfax – a distance of fifty-one miles – the scenery is in many places grand beyond conception. We are not on the highest lands of the Sierras by any means, for bleak and bare of verdure rise the granite peaks around us. Piles of granite, their weather-stained and snow-clad sides glistening in the morning sun, rise between us and the western shore. Scattering groups of hardy fir and spruce line the mountain gorges, where also rest the everlasting snows. There is, perhaps, no grander scenery in the Sierras – of towering mountains, deep gorges, lofty precipices, sparkling waterfalls, and crystal lakes – than abounds along this road to Colfax. From the time the road enters the crest of the summit it passes through a succession of tunnels and snow-sheds so closely connected that we can hardly tell when the cars enter or leave a tunnel. The Summit Tunnel, the largest of the number, is 1659 feet long, the others ranging from 100 to 870 feet in length. Fires often cause great damage to the snow-sheds. Just lately a portion of them were burnt, and the smouldering cinders can yet be seen. Leaving the summit we pass on through snow-sheds and tunnels, around the base of the towering peaks, anon over the bare ridge, with an unbroken view on either hand, then amid grand old forest trees until we reach the cascades six miles west of the summit. Here we cross one of the branches of the Yuba, which goes leaping down the rocks in a shower of spray. Passing on we turn up Blue Canyon, the road on the opposite bank apparently running parallel with the one we are traversing. At Blue Canyon an observation car was attached to our train, and from it a good view was obtained of the beauties yet to come. We swung around the head of the Canyon, past saw-mills and lumber side tracks. Still speeding on, we leave Blue Canyon, its sporting waters, and giant pines, pass China Ranch, Shady Run and Alta.

Still further on is Dutch Flat and Gold Run – gold mining towns. Passing on we finally come to Cape Horn. This, I think, is the grandest scene on this whole line of the trans-continental railroad. Now we turn sharp around to our right, where the towering mass of rock have been cut down, affording a road-bed where a few years ago the savage could not make a foot track. Far above us they rear their black crests, towering away, as it were, to the clouds, while the valley on our left is a thousand feet below us still – some say two thousand. Passing on four miles below Cape Horn, we arrive at Colfax, and with a sad heart bid adieu to the beauties of the Sierras, of which we only got a faint panoramic view.

After leaving Colfax, we rapidly passed over the beautiful and fertile plains and hills of the State of California, covered with many pretty homesteads. Much could be said of this State, but space will not permit. Passing Sacramento City, with its 16,000 inhabitants, unnoticed, we finally arrived at San Francisco on the evening of the 3rd of July. We have travelled from the far east to the far west – from where the sun rises out of the waters to where it sets in the water, covering an extent of country 3,263 miles in width.

CHAPTER II

San Francisco – Voyage to Portland, Oregon – Columbia River – Portland – Nature and Art – Sail to Monticello, Washington Territory – Staging to Olympia – Big Trees – Mound Prairie – Olympia – Puget Sound

---

The history of San Francisco is so well known that any particular mention would be mono-tonous. However, there are many things of interest of which I might speak, but only a few of them I shall notice. It has an area of about eight square miles, and, according to the last census, a population of 178,000 inhabitants. It is stated that it has the mildest and most equable climate known to any large city in the world. In January, the coldest month, the mean temperature is fifty degrees, while the mean temperature of September, the warmest month, is fifty-eight degrees, giving an average difference of only eight or nine degrees in the variations of the entire year. The average temperature of the whole year is fifty-four degrees. The city presents a broken appear-ance, owing to a portion being built on the hills, which attain quite respectable altitudes.

The first house built in San Francisco was in 1835. The place was then called Yuba Buena, changed to San Francisco in 1847, *before the discovery of gold.* Then five hundred white settlers could not be found in as many hundred miles, and not one ship a year visited this bay. One is almost lost in wonder and astonishment, when we look back only 25 years and see what a won-derful change has taken place on the Pacific coast, and especially here in this *city by the sea.*

San Francisco is amply supplied with schools, both public and private. There are 46 churches – of all kinds, creeds and beliefs – including several Chinese 'Joss Houses.' There are in the city 60 newspapers, magazines and periodicals. Several streets are occupied by the Chinese, and the place is called China Town, and there the Celestials rule supreme. But we must not linger here too long, but pass on our journey.

We failed to get to this city in time to connect with the regular steamer for Victoria. We, how-ever, ascertained that the steamer *John L. Stephens* would sail on the 6th of July for Port-land, Oregon, and that there we could connect with another steamer for Victoria. After spend-ing three days pleasuring in San Francisco we sailed on the 6th in the above steamer, and after a very rough passage of four and a-half days we arrived on the 10th of July at Portland, Oregon. This city is on the Willamette River about 12 miles from its confluence with the Columbia, or 112 miles from the mouth of the latter river. The scenes on each side of the Columbia, as far as St. Helen, are very fine indeed. Much of the way is bestudded with islands. Now we enter a narrow channel, and looking forward we scarcely know how the ship is to get out, for all we see on every hand is land. But soon the command *Hard to port* is heard, when the ship gracefully moves around a spit and we again emerge forth into the main channel of the river some 5 or 6 miles wide. Still further up we get the first glimpse of Mount St. Helen, clad with everlasting snows. It appears to be but 30 or 40 miles from us, but I am told that it is at least 160 miles from St. Helen Village, and is 12,000 feet high. St. Helen is a small village about 80 miles from the mouth of the Columbia. Soon after passing it we come to what is called the still waters of the Columbia. Looking to our left we suddenly come in sight of the ever memorable Mount Hood, rising majestically 14,700 feet. At the same time by looking across the stern of the boat we are still in sight of Mount St. Helen. The Columbia as far as the Willemette River is noted for its salmon fisheries. Indeed nothing but fishing villages, stations and huts can be seen. It appears strange, after seeing nothing but a dense forest on each side of the river – except the above fisheries – suddenly to come in sight of a large and prosperous city like Portland. A few years since this spot was a wild forest, the home of the grizzly bear and other ugly beasts. But now Portland boasts of having 12,000 or 15,000 inhabitants, many large and substantial buildings, wide streets and not a few paved with the Nicholson pavement. The country, for a considerable distance around it, is well settled and cultivated. In the rear of the city is a high mountain, a zigzag road leading to its top where is an old deserted hut, surrounded with all kinds of fruit trees. Here is the cherry, bending with ripe delicious fruit, apples and pears promise an abundant crop; currants, raspberries, blackberries, grapes, etc., grow seemingly without any special culture. And what may I say of *roses.* Everywhere roses may be seen, – roses in profusion.

Sitting on the porch of the hut, I have a beautiful view of the city and river which lie hundreds of feet below me. In the far distance, a little east of north, I again see Mount St. Helen, and a little north of east the famous Mount Hood. The scene is very enticing, so much so that after sitting two hours I still loved to linger. Here in one view are art and nature beautifully blended together. Here and yonder are the everlasting mountains, hills and vales, covered with the lofty pine and fir trees, and the ripening grain. In the valley beneath, – the Willamette, bestudded with many islands, flows gently on towards the northern star. In these I see nature, the works of Him who spake and it was done. At my feet, by the river, is the city, with its broad and beautiful streets – ornamented with trees, – princely mansions, halls, and churches with towering domes. There in the river lay great ships which defy the storm of the sea. There is the iron horse rushing on with its long train of cars; in these I see art, the works of man, who, using the materials God gave him, made many things, great, grand and wonderful. Yet, when compared with Dame Nature, the majestic work of God, all this artistic transformation sinks almost into utter oblivion.

'Lovely, indeed, the mimic works of art,
    But nature's works far lovelier.'

The steamer in which we had to sail from Portland to Victoria had ceased to run, so we made arrangements to go by the overland route to Olympia, on Puget Sound, and from there, by steamer, sail down the sound, and across the strait of Juan de Fuca to Victoria, Vancouver's Island. Therefore, after spending a few days very pleasantly in Portland, we went on board the steamer *Rescue,* on the morning of the 14th of July, and sailed down the Willamette river to the Columbia; down the Columbia to the mouth of Cowlitz River and up this stream to Monticello, in Washington territory, altogether a distance of 55 miles. We arrived at noon of the same day, and soon after left in a stage for Olympia – a distance of 90 miles. After travelling 15 miles we arrived at Castle Rock, a post station, kept by Mr. Wm. Jackson. Here we stopped for the night. Berries of all kinds grow here in abundance, and after getting rid of some of the dust by brushing and washing, we all went up on the hills, and ate berries of our own picking to our fill. Here, also, grow the largest trees I ever saw. While we were on the hills, I measured one three feet above ground, which proved to be 29 feet in circumference, and I think about 300 feet high. Upon returning to the station, Mr. Jackson spoke of a stump of a tree, standing in his meadow, but a short distance from his house, which is 45 feet in girth. Mr. Hammond and I expressed a desire to see it, so Jackson led the way and soon we were at the famous *stump.* The bark had already disappeared, and the stump was considerably *burnt.* I measured it 3½ feet above ground, and found it to be exactly 50 feet in circumference. What it was in its primitive state, when it was covered with thick bark, can scarcely now be conjectured. As it is, its bark would enclose a room 17 feet in diameter. The meadow in which we found the stump, is also worthy of note. It is a beautiful timothy meadow, the grass of which is on an average four and a half feet high, and stood very thick on the ground. The next day we made an early start, crossed Pomroy Mountains, and passed over very rough, hilly roads, and through forests of the largest pine and fir trees. The greater part of these, however, were burnt about 20 years ago, and the dead trunks remain standing giving the hills and mountains a desolate appearance. Yet they remind us of their primeval glory. Late in the evening of the 15th of July we arrived at the Half-way House, and stopped for the night. A few minutes before we arrived at this house we crossed the Shookum Chack River, which empties into the Chehalis not more than three-fourths of a mile from here. In the afternoon of Sunday, July 16th, we arrived at Olympia, sore, tired, and all covered with dust. At times, as we were journeying on, we were almost suffocated with dust. One of the bystanders at Olympia had the coolness to say to Mr. Richardson, as he was alighting from the coach: – 'Old man, your face is dirty.' Of course it was meant, and taken, in merriment over our wretched plight. But after a wholesome dusting and bathing, we were ready for dinner. After dinner we placed our baggage on board the steamer North Pacific, and also took berths in it for the night.

There are numerous settlements along the road from Monticello to Olympia, and many of them are quite new. Wherever any attempt at farming is made everything seems to grow luxuriantly. The best grass and grain fields, of every description, I ever saw lie along this road. About eight miles before we came to Olympia we passed through a strange plain. It may most properly be called 'Mound Prairie.' The whole prairie or plain – some two miles long and one wide – is covered with mounds. These are from 5 to 7 feet high, about 20 feet in diameter, and very regular in formation. The majority of them are in tiers or rows, as regularly laid out as the streets of a city, and I think about 10 feet apart. This may be an old Indian burying ground, but I am told that as yet nothing has been found in them.

Olympia is a small village of about 1,500 inhabitants, and beautifully situated at the head of Puget Sound. It has certainly many attractions, and will no doubt ere long become a thriving city. Here I met a Mr. Macleay, formerly of Montreal. He is a wholesale grocer, and is doing a thriving business. By his kindness we were led across a bridge three-fourths of a mile long, leading across an arm of the Sound, and up a high hill. Here we had a beautiful view of the Sound and Village in the foreground, and the snow-clad Mount Rainier in the background. This Mount is I understand 60 miles from here and 10,000 feet high.

At four o'clock, on the morning of the 17th of July, we sailed down Puget Sound on our way to Victoria, crossed San Juan Strait, and arrived at the above place at 9 p.m.[1] There are but very few settlements along Puget Sound. It is lined on each side by forests of the largest timber. A few places boast of a thousand inhabitants, among which are Seattle and Port Townsend.

Aside from these there are a few large lumbering places or stations at which we stopped. Upon the whole Puget Sound is a beautiful sheet of water. On the right we are in almost continual view of the Cascade range of mountains, and on the left are the rugged peaks and bluffs of the Olympian range. Both of these are covered with perpetual snow.

CHAPTER III

Victoria – Confederation Day – Wives Wanted – Sail to Yale – New Westminster – Fraser River – Yale – The Scenery at Yale – Indian Salmon Fishing and Curing – Canadian Pacific R.R. Survey – Walk to Litton

The Gazette, June 27, 1872

We were all more or less disappointed in our expectations of Victoria, Vancouver's Island. I expected (judging from reports) to find a thriving and enterprising city, with prosperity written upon it every where. But I was grieved to find everything the reverse of prosperity. Some streets are nearly entirely deserted, and there is not a street but what has many, very many, houses – both dwellings and stores – deserted. Everything looks lifeless and desolate. Its population does not exceed 3,500. During the gold excitement of 1864 and 1865 in Cariboo and other places it had a population of 10,000. Then every house was occupied, and yet there were many without shelter, so that hundreds of tents were erected upon vacant lots and in the suburbs. But in a few years the gold excitement died away, and with it went the sudden increase of population. The natural location of Victoria is exceedingly beautiful, and can scarcely be excelled for a large and beautiful city. Nature has done everything for it. The harbour, though not large, is very good. The scenery, also, is very fine, being in full view of the snow-clad Cascade and Olympian Ranges of Mountains. The climate is delightful. Heat and cold are at no time in extreme. In summer, the dry season – it scarcely ever rains. In the winter, the *wet* season, they expect much rain, yet it does not continually pour down rain, as some would

1 Selwyn says July 10, but it is obviously a typographical error. Selwyn, 'Journal and Report,' 20.

suppose. The greater part of the rain falls during the night, and often the days are very pleasant, even in the rainy or winter season. Snow and ice are almost strangers here. The same, as to climate, might be said of the greater part of Vancouver's Island.

Upon the morning of the 20th of July – about midnight – I was wakened from a sound sleep by the ringing of bells, exploding of fire-crackers, Roman candles, bursting of sky-rockets, hurrahs, and shouting of every description. In my first dreamish fancy I imagined that we were about to be consumed by a great conflagration; but in a moment it occurred to me that it was *'Confederation Day,'* and thus at this early hour the Victorians began to celebrate the day. This day the Dominion of Canada, British Columbia, and Vancouver's Island got married, and became one. Frequently we heard the Victorians say: – *'We are Canadians now.'* There seemed to be a great deal of unanimity about the matter. Although after the midnight salute, there was nothing of interest present during the day, except two picnics, one by the Methodist Sunday-School and the other by the Mechanics' Institute. The latter was kept up till quite a late hour in the night.

To me everything seems to be done in a strange way in Victoria. The postal system was all out of gear. The office was only open when the mail came in, and that was about two or three times a week, and no one seemed to know what the postage was to any place. But the Dominion will soon arrange this matter. (After returning from the mountains, we found the postal system in perfect working order.) The eating of this place is also peculiar. If a person has plenty of time, and any amount of patience, he will get something good at the Colonial House. We almost invariably got bread here by the yard or half yard. Among other novelties I found the good intent of advertising for a wife to be in vogue, of which the following

is a sample, which I clipped from the *Standard:*
WANTED A WIFE – Mr. Samuel Ricketts, of Mount Farm, Lake District, having a good farm and being free from debt, on which he milks eighteen cows, wants to get married to a girl of good character who can manage a dairy, and who is tolerably good-looking and not over 32 years of age. Letters left at the *Standard* office will be attended to.
Mr. Ricketts was still free and in a marrying humor when I last saw him, so there is yet a chance for a 'tolerably good-looking' maiden.

I saw many Indians here, but of these and others I will speak after I know more of their habits, way of life, etc.

After spending a few days in Victoria, viewing and preparing for our expedition into the interior,* we sailed about 10 a.m. of the 25th of July in the steamer *Enterprise* for New Westminster on the Fraser River, distance eighty miles. It was very calm, and we had a very pleasant sail through the Straits, Gulf of Georgia, and up the Fraser River, to the above place, arriving there at 6 p.m. of the same day, and stopping at the Colonial Hotel. New Westminster, the former Capital of British Columbia is a very small village, situated by the side of a steep hill. It has only a few hundred inhabitants, and a large number of Indians. The country around it is a dense forest of the largest timber.

Misquetoes abound here abundantly, and were very desirous to make our acquaintance. But I am sure we did not relish the style of their introduction. We were serenaded by them during the night, and, as compensation for their services, [they] required some of our blood. But we had all been bled more or less, before, by sharpers on the way, and had to endure them also. Our party – the geological – were not the only party sailing on the steamer. The railroad surveying party for British Columbia were also on board, numbering about seventy-five men. Mr. R. McLennan[2] and Mr. Moberly[3] being the District Civil Engineers, and head[s]

* Plates 1-8

2 Roderick McLennan (1842- ?). Born in Ontario, served with the C.P.R Surveys and subsequently became a railway contractor building one of the difficult Lake Superior sections. He was later a banker and held directorships in a number of large companies. He was elected to Parliament as a Conservative in 1891.

3 Walter Moberly (1832-1915). Born in England, Moberly was educated as an engineer at Toronto. He went to British Columbia in 1858 where he supervised construction of the Cariboo Wagon Road. While Assistant Surveyor-General of British Columbia in 1865-1866 he discovered Eagle Pass. In 1870 he was made a District Civil Engineer in charge of several parties performing mountain surveys for the C.P.R. Surveys.

of the parties.

Early on the morning of the next day we embarked in the river steamer *Lillooet*, and continued our course up the river. By 10 p.m. we arrived at Port Hope – having travelled eighty-five miles – and stopped in the boat for the night.[4] Hope is but a small village of a few hundred inhabitants on the east bank of the Fraser, and without any special interest. At early dawn of the 26th of July the steamer left her mooring at Hope, and continued her course up the river. At 7 a.m. we arrived at Yale – the head of navigation on the Fraser River, 100 miles above New Westminster.[5]

The country along the lower end of the Fraser River is very low, level, and rather marshy. Near the mouth of the river it is frequently flooded by the high tide. It, however, gradually rises until we get within twenty miles of Hope, when we near the Cascade range of mountains. Gradually the scenery increases in beauty, grandeur and interest. And as we near Yale, bold bluffs, walls of rocks and mountains arise majestically on each side, and we are evidently entering the Cascades. Before we arrive at New Westminster, and between this and Hope, there are a number of small settlements, and men, I hear, are doing well.

Yale is an interesting little place of about six hundred inhabitants, a few Chinamen, and at the upper end a large Indian village. It is interesting on account of its locality. It is, however, impossible for it ever to become a very large place, for it is hemmed in almost on every side by mountains of rock rising almost perpendicularly. From here to the gold regions at Cariboo there is a good stage road, – good especially at this season of the year. Mr. Barnard has a stage and express line running on this road to Cariboo. The view, looking up this river, is indescribably grand. This is the entrance of the Fraser Canyon through the Cascade Mountains. The lower Canyon is about half a mile from Yale, and as we approach near it, we see walls, or mountains of rock piled on each other, on either side of the river, rising almost perpendicular thousands of feet high. Here and there small mountain streams came rushing and leaping down in a shower of spray. On the left bank or in the wall of rocks, the Cariboo road is cut, in many places the rocks projecting over the road, and in other places bridges spanning – from rock to rock – across the small gorges which seem the brow of those rugged bluffs. Beneath, the Fraser rushes, roaring and thundering through the Canyon. In the centre of this boiling flood rises a large rock which is about 100 feet long, 50 feet wide and 40 feet high.

At the foot of the Canyon, on each side of the river, the Indians have fastened scaffolding to the rocks, extending over the boiling water. Upon this they stand and fish for salmon with large meshed nets fastened to an oval hoop or bow, and this to a long pole. This net they run down into an eddy by the rocks, and when the salmon becomes entangled in the net, his leaps warn the fisherman of the fact. The current, even in the eddy, is so strong that the Indians have the end of their nets tied to a long rope which is fastened to the rocks below, and thus they are kept from being washed away. In this way they take a great many salmon, and most of them quite large, averaging, I think, about ten pounds each. The catching is the work of the Indians, and the cleaning and curing is the work of the squaws. After a faint attempt at taking off the scales, the fish is cut open on the back, however only cutting half way down, and then splitting the flesh on each side, thus forming one piece of the two sides. The meat of this is now cut crossways in strips of about an inch in width, but only to the skin, and then hung up to dry. The rest of the fish is similarly dealt with after taking out the entrails. In this

4 Selwyn says 9 P.M. Selwyn, 'Journal and Report,' 21.
5 Selwyn says 8 A.M. Ibid.

116

way they prepare large quantities at this season of the year for their winter use, and the stench arising therefrom is in many places to us almost unendurable.

The Canadian Pacific Railroad survey divided themselves into two divisions, one under charge of District Engineer Moberly, and one under charge of District Engineer R. McLennan. These were again sub-divided; the former into Co.T., Mr. Jollette, C.E., in charge, who was directed to go to Kamloop[6] and survey a route to Howe's Pass.[7] And Co.S., Mr. Moan,[8] C.E., in charge, who is to examine Shooswap Lake and Eagle Pass. Mr. McLennan's division was also divided into Co.R. Mr. Mahood, C.E., in charge, and Co.Q – Mr. Green,[9] C.E., in charge. Co.R is to go to Cariboo, and work their way eastward to Cranberry Lake and Co.Q. is to go to Kamloop, up the North Thompson river, pass Cranberry Lake through Leather Pass, on to the Jasper House on the east of the Rocky Mountains. Moan's party stopped at Hope and commenced their operations there. Mahood went to Cariboo by stage, and there commenced his work. The other two companies will go to Kamloop, which will be the base of their operations. Mr. McLennan determined to go along with Mr. Green's party, and Mr. Moberly to accompany Co.T. Mr. Mahood was in Yale in advance of us, and obtained nearly all the means of transportation that Mr. Bernard possessed. So the men of Companies Q. and T. had to walk to Savona Ferry, on Komloop Lake, distance 135 miles. Under these circumstances Mr. Selwyn thought it best for us to walk and get four Indians to carry what things we needed on the way, and send the balance by Bernard's Express. He had engaged one man at Victoria, and the four Indians made our party at this time *nine* in number.

Every thing being arranged we left Yale at 7 a.m. of July 28th, and started on our foot expedition to Kamloop Lake. This day we walked 13 miles, and camped at the Suspension Bridge.[10]

Early the next day we were again on the way and travelled 17 miles and camped at Butcher's Flat. Twelve miles from the Suspension Bridge is Boston Bar. Being much fatigued we stopped to rest and ate a good dinner. The day was very hot, 85 degrees in the shade and 110 in the sun.[11]

The following day being Sunday (July 30th) we rested, and it is well we did, for the heat was almost unendurable – thermometer 99° in the shade.

By 5.45 a.m. on July 31st we were again on the way, and by 6 p.m. we were at Lytton, which is at the confluence of the Fraser and Thompson rivers.[12] The distance we walked this day was 27 miles, and I was foot sore, limb sore and perfectly *give out*. I, however, was not the only one; we all suffered about equally from fatigue. The heat was intense, being again 99 degrees in the shade. In the sun I cannot say, my thermometer only reading 130 degrees, and the mercury arose as far as it could above this indication. Mr. Selwyn declared that he would walk no further, so he discharged the Indians, two of them having already given out, and telegraphed to Bernard and engaged a stage which had just arrived from Cariboo empty.

ERRATUM – In speaking of Mound Prairie, in Chapter 2nd, read about *eight* miles, &c., and not eighty, as printed.

6 Kamloops.
7 i.e. Howse Pass.
8 Edward Mohun.
9 Probably Ashdown Green.
10 Alexandria Suspension Bridge built by Joseph Trutch.
11 Selwyn says 80° in the shade and 105° in the sun. Selwyn, 'Journal and Report,' 22.
12 Selwyn says 6:30 A.M. Ibid.

CHAPTER IV

Fraser Canyon – Old Mule Trail – China-
man's Bluff – Indian Chief's Grave – Bad
Man's Rock – The Young Chief – Jackass
Mountain – Lytton – Staging to Savona
Ferry – Freight Teams – Hail Storm – Sail
to Kamloop – Tranquill Mills – Battle Bluff

The Gazette, July 1, 1872

Having now a little leisure – while waiting for
the stage – I will return and describe some of
the scenes, etc., which we passed on the way
from Yale.

Words cannot express the grandeur and sublimity of the scenery in the Fraser Canyon. To
describe its charms would occupy more space
and time than I can afford. At each step the
scene changes, like a grand living panorama, as
it is, whose architect and artist is the Great I
Am. On each side of us rise tall gigantic buttresses of black looking rocks thousands of feet
above us, whose very frown inspires us with
awe, as we slowly ascend the Canyon.

Looking across the Canyon at the almost
perpendicular cliffs on our right, (and also on
our left), we see a number of dwarf pine trees,
moderating the sternness of the landscape and
by their beautiful green foliage, relieving the
sombre hue of the mountain side. Higher up,
on the summit, the snow reigns supreme, and
by its whiteness, causes the foliage of the pine
trees to assume a dark appearance. Beneath us,
on our right, there is a yawning chasm in the
bottom of which the waters of the Fraser and
the boulders are at war, as the river rushes
along as if in haste to escape from its gloomy
prison walls, to bask in the sunshine beyond.

About eight miles from Yale we crossed
Spuzzam River,[13] a beautiful stream of pure
crystal water.* As seen from the Cariboo road it
looked very peculiar.

The Suspension Bridge,* – 13 miles from
Yale, – is a beautifully constructed wire bridge
with large wooden abutments, painted white.
It spans the Fraser, the width being 350 feet. It
was built by Gov. Trutch,[14] who at first collected
toll, but it now belongs to the Government and
the crossing is free. The scenery around the
bridge is very fine, but as we ascend the Fraser
it momentarily increases in beauty, grandeur
and interest.

About three miles from this bridge the road
begins to ascend a steep grade until it rises
about 500 feet above the bed of the river. Here
the road bed is cut in the side of the almost
perpendicular rocks; they extending over the
road about 10 feet. About 50 feet above this is
the old mule trail, also cut in the side of the
Bluff. Curiosity led me to go a little further up
the road where the Bluff is less steep and climb
up to this trail. I found it to be only five feet
wide, and along this dangerous path the mule
trains used to travel carrying from 300 to 500
pounds each. If any of them should stumble,
sudden death awaited them, as the perpendicular height from the trail to the rocks and
river beneath is fully 500 feet. Above this the
rocks rise cragged and bleak to the enormous
height of 4000 feet. Descending we came to
Hell's Gate in the Fraser.

This seems to be the climax of boldness and
grandeur in the Fraser canyon. It is by far the
most fearful rapid. On each side the rocks rise
in square and rectangular blocks and columns,
like a vast piece of masonry. Between this narrow chasm the water tumbles and tosses
through with a deafening noise. A little below
the gate a perpendicular wall of rocks extends
from the road into the river, about 150 feet
long, from 3 to 10 feet in thickness, and 200
feet high, leaving a chasm between it and the
main rock of 12 feet wide and 200 feet deep.

* Plate 11
* Plates 12 & 13
13 i.e. Spuzzum River.
14 Joseph William Trutch (1826-1904). Born in England, where he was trained as a civil engineer, he
went to California in 1849. In 1859 he went to
British Columbia where he worked on the
Cariboo wagon road and built the Alexandria
Suspension Bridge across the Fraser River. He
was one of three delegates who negotiated the
terms of union with Canada and he became first
Lieutenant-Governor of British Columbia serv-
ing 1871-1876. He was knighted in 1889.

From Hell's Gate we again begin to ascend another bluff, named Chinaman's Bluff. At the highest point is a bridge spanning a fearful gorge extending from the mountain, thousands of feet above, to the river, 900 feet below us. On each end of the bridge the rocks are cut away, affording a passage for the road. The descent on the upper side of this bluff is very steep. Soon after we descended, I saw on my right the grave of an Indian chief. I went up to it, and found it to be a great novelty to me. I examined it closely, and upon inquiry I am able to give the following particulars: Under the front of a large clap-board shed, closed only by the roof and back, is a large *black canoe,* with white figures painted on the sides. The chief, when he dies, is doubled up, his knees to his chin, and his arms tied across the lower part of his legs. In this position he is placed in a box just large enough to receive him. This is then placed in the canoe. A few of his robes or skins are placed over the box, and then covered with clap-boards and left to decay. All the chief's effects go with him to the grave. In this case, four high poles are raised in front of the shed, and some smaller ones fastened acrosss them. To each upright is fastened a colored cloth, white, red, green, and blue. His horse and two mules were killed, and their skins hung across the poles. Here also are his guns, hanging on the pole, with the locks off. Here hangs his royal robe or suit, banners, shawls, blankets, etc. Part of his robes, skins, and blankets, are packed with him in this canoe, and all left to moulder and decay with him. Formerly when a chief of the Douglas tribe died (which is the tribe of which I am now speaking) it was customary to kill four or five of his slaves, so that their spirits might accompany the chief to his new hunting ground. The Government has forbidden this practice, and now, in order to keep up the spirit of the custom, they carve out a few wooden images, and place them at the grave. Here there are four; two as canoemen, each having an Indian paddle. The other two represent youths standing by the canoe, with hands in pockets. The images are dressed in a fashion with red and white cotton cloth.

Behind this canoe are a few more objects of interest and curiosity. In the centre of the shed is a large hole like a grave, the sides of which are boarded up with clap-boards, and then lined with rush matting. It is empty, with the exception of a roll or two of matting. This is for the reception of the chief's bones after he and his effects have decayed. In each end of the shed are two other graves. These contain relatives of the chief.

Ordinarily these Indians are buried by placing the corpse in a box, as above described, and then burying it in the ground, and sometimes only placing it on the ground and covered with boards. All their effects are placed at the grave with them. The missionaries are labouring amongst them, and no doubt they will finally change their custom of burial, as they become civilized.

About half a mile up the road from this grave is an Indian village of considerable size, situated at the confluence of the Fraser and Anderson Rivers. Passing it, and crossing the latter river on a long bridge we soon came to Boston Bar. After dining and resting, we passed on to Butcher's Flat without witnessing any peculiar scenes.

About a mile further on from Butcher's Flat, looking across the river, on our left, we see near the river a high conical rock projecting out of the mountain side. It is about 40 feet high, standing solitary and alone among the green pine trees. The Indians have a curious tradition with regard to this rock. They say, that long, long ago there were two men travelling along this river, one a very good man, and the other very bad. The good man tried to go to Heaven, but the bad man hindered him, and laid every obstacle in his way, so the good man changed his evil companion to stone, and here it has stood ever since as a warning and rebuke, while he (the good man) is gone to Heaven, or the *new hunting ground,* and is basking in its sunny shores eternally.

Soon after passing this Bad Man's Rock, we again begin to ascend, to cross, in this instance, between a bluff extending into a great bend of the Fraser and Main Mountain. As I was slowly ascending, in advance of the party, I passed a large company of Indians coming down, their horses laden with black moss, of which I will speak hereafter. Giving the usual greeting of *Klahowya,'* (How do you do) I passed on. Soon after I saw an Indian youth coming down the hill towards me. Drawing near, with a friendly, smiling countenance, he spoke and saluted me with *Klahowya.'* I replied in his own language. Then in broken English he asked me: 'Where you from?' I told him from the far east or sunrise. His next question was, 'Where go you?' After telling him, he again asked, 'What for?' I told him as best I could, and now thinking it was my turn to be inquisitive, I asked him, 'What he was? Where he go? What that ornamental sham bag he wore meant? etc,' to which he replied, 'I am Chief. I go home. Live at the foot of mountain. Those Indians I passed, some of my people. This bag is an insignia of my office as chief.' After wishing him to be a *skookum tumtum kloshe* TYEE *kopa mika tilikum,* (a brave man and good chief to his people.) I bid him *klahowya'* and passed on. [...]¹⁵ between bluff and mountain, I stopped till my fellow travellers caught up. Here on the right is a bakery, on the left is an Indian camp, – part of the young chief's tribe, – a little further on is the Forest House, kept by Boothroyd & Bro. Soon after passing the 42nd mile house, which is near the foot of the mountain we just crossed, we came to a large mountain stream falling over the almost perpendicular rocks on our right. The height of the falls is about 350 feet. It is upon the whole quite picturesque. From this fall the road again begins to ascend, this time to cross along the rugged sides of Jackass Mountain. Certainly this is the most romantic part of the road over which we have as yet travelled. At the highest point of the road is a bridge crossing a deep narrow mountain gorge, or chasm. From this bridge a grand view can be enjoyed if one has the *nerve* to stand at the lower or river side of the bridge. It is really something fearful to look down this rugged chasm, extending to the river a thousand feet below. One grows giddy at the sight of this fearful height, especially upon the first view. But we soon forget ourselves, and all danger, as we become enraptured with the grandeur of the scene before us. Here, standing upon the verge of this precipice and looking down upon the valley 1,000 feet below, we see the Fraser, like a slender silver thread, winding along on its course. As seen from here one would not suppose it to be the turbulent waters of the mighty Fraser, warring with every obstacle which may come in its way. Opposite the mountain gently rises for many thousand feet. Its sides are covered, scatteringly, with pine trees. Behind us the cragged rocks of Jackass Mountain, rise high above us and shut out our view in that direction. There is no traveller or tourist who, viewing the grand picture spread out before him as he stands on the Jackass Mountain bridge, is so dead to the grand and the sublime in nature, but he will carry along with him a life-long recollection of its imposing magnificence. It is quite impossible to do it justice by any description. It was with reluctance that I left this spot. Between this and Lytton there was nothing worthy to note.

Lytton is a very small village, 57 miles from Yale.* Most of the houses are unpainted one story wooden buildings. It has a grist mill, several stores, groceries, and a few hotels. Its

* Plates 14 & 15
15 One line cut off at bottom of page of newspaper original.

120

inhabitants are composed of two-thirds whites and one-third Indians and Chinamen. The soil is light and sandy, and the wind blows unceasingly almost like a hurricane, and one can imagine the effect of sand and dust.

On the morning of the 2nd of August we took the stage and travelled 23 miles to Cook's Ferry, on the Thompson River. The next day we went to Bonaparte River, and passed much beautiful scenery, having travelled 30 miles. The mountains, however, are no longer so high; we have now fairly passed through the Cascade range. From Lytton the pine trees become smaller and fewer in number as we leave the Fraser and ascend the Thompson River. Here at Bonaparte there are scarcely any trees. Here and there a dwarf pine may be seen, but principally sandy hills, covered more or less with wild sage, and bunch grass.

There are numerous freight teams travelling this road, carrying freight to Cariboo and other localities on the road.* The teamsters generally have two waggons coupled together, in which they carry from seven to ten tons. They are drawn by 12 or 14 mules, or by 16 to 20 bullocks. In going up the steep grades they separate the waggons and take one up at a time, and then couple them again.

In the afternoon of August 4th we had a very warm and dusty drive to Savona Ferry,* which is at the outlet of Kamloop lake into the Thompson River.[16] Here we pitched our tents, 'for there was no room in the inn,' it being already occupied by the railroad survey. Mr. Selwyn and Moberly hired a canoe and a few Indians, and started for Kamloop, and we, Mr. Richardson, Hammond, Dean, and I, remained here till our provisions, etc, arrived from Yale. The next day Mr. Richardson and I took a small boat and rowed up the lake about three miles, prospecting. The whole day was very warm, but at 5:30 p.m. we had a heavy hail storm. The first gusts of wind brought clouds

of dust and sand. This being the dry season, and the soil of the whole country here a dry, sandy mould, sparsely covered with sage brush and more or less bunch grass, anyone can imagine the fearful dust that a wind storm will produce upon dry sandy hills and valleys like this. Our experience proves it to be something fearful. The first blast of wind, aside from bringing clouds of dust, blew Mr. Richardson's tent down. Before the hail and rain came, there was a short lull in the storm, and we hastily re-pitched the tent again. No sooner was it put up than the storm came upon us in all its fury. Our tents, after a little bracing, stood the storm nobly. It was quite a novelty sitting under a tent in a hail storm, with the wind blowing like a furious hurricane; the tent curtains flapping; the rain pouring down, intermixed with the thudding of the large hail stones; the lightning flashing; the sharp and receding thunder roaring; the uproar and noise of the hail and wind on the lake; all made an impression upon me not easily to be forgotten.

Our stock of goods arriving we hired a small five ton boat and sailed on the morning of the 8th of Aug. for Kamloop, which is at the confluence of the north and south Thompson rivers. The Indian word 'Kamloop' means 'the meeting of the waters,' and thus it is a very appropriate name.

The wind was contrary so we made but little progress. By noon we only made seven miles, so we went to shore and made a lunch by baking dampers, frying bacon, and boiling tea. While these were preparing I walked along the shore and found a few nice agates. After lunch we again tried to sail, but were not out long when a cold rain storm came upon us. We made an attempt to outride the waves, but the sea became too rough for the small boat, and there was much danger of her getting swamped, for the waves at times dashed over into the vessel. So we turned the boat and sailed before the

* Plates 21 & 22
* Plate 23
16 Selwyn says August 5. Selwyn, 'Journal and Report,' 24.

wind, and ran into a small cove. It was well we did, for the storm became more furious than ever. With the storm came cold, and we were all shivering. After the storm abated we again took to our boat, but only went to Tranquille Mills at the mouth of Tranquille river,* distance from Savona Ferry 18 miles. This is the first mill in this region of the country, and is certainly a quaint-looking frontier mill, owned by Mr. Wm. Fortune. He and family were very kind to us. They put in a large fire in their kitchen stove and had us take a good drying and warming and in the meantime they prepared for us a good supper – of course for a consideration. This was the first good meal we had for two weeks, and we all did justice to it. What made it still better, Mrs. Fortune was at the head of the table and served without stint.

Soon after supper we rolled ourselves up in our blankets on the 'soft side of the floor,' (Fortune's having no extra beds), and soon forgot all our day's troubles. The next morning we had a favourable wind, so we made an early start and were not long in sailing the seven miles up the Thompson to Kamloop, which is 340 miles from Victoria.

Kamloop Lake is a beautiful sheet of water laying between hills and mountains. It is about 18 miles long and 6 miles wide. The waters of the Thompson river run through it, and a few minor streams empty into it, among which is Tranquille River. Near the mouth of this stream there are several interesting scenes, among which is Battle Bluff, and the serrated or basaltic rocks near to it.* The Bluff rises, as it were, out of the waters of the lake to an almost perpendicular height of 1,000 feet. Here, at the foot of this rock, a naval battle was fought about a hundred years ago between two Indian tribes, – at least so the Indians say. The victorious tribe stained or painted a large projecting rock, which is about 15 feet above water, with some kind of red material to commemorate the

place. Many of the present Indians have superstitious notions in relation to this place. The Bluff had no name, although it is the most prominent point on the lake, so we named it Battle Bluff.

CHAPTER V

Photographing at Kamloop Lake – H.B. Steamer – Unexpected Rains – Departure of Companies Q. & T. of the R.R. Survey – Country from the Mouth of the Fraser River to Kamloop – Kamloop – Mr. J. Richardson's Departure – Our party

The Gazette, July 3, 1872

Having to remain a few days in Kamloop to prepare a train for our journey up the North Thompson, and to hire a few more men, gave me a good opportunity for viewing. Selwyn borrowed a boat for us, so Hammond, Dean and I sailed down the river to the lake on a short photographing expedition. We made our headquarters, for a few days, at Tranquille Mills, and received much kindness from Mrs. Fortune.

The nights were very warm, and the mosquitoes kept up a continual hubbub, so that we could not sleep. We tried to smoke them out of the cabin we occupied, but no use, the indefatigable fellows would come, and they were so very large 'that *many* of them weighed a pound.'

After spending a few days viewing along the shores of Kamloop Lake and up Tranquille River, which is but a very small stream, we started back to Kamloop on the evening of August 12th. We had a fair wind when we left Tranquille Mills, but did not sail more than three-fourths of a mile when we were be-

* Plate 24
* Plates 25-27

122

calmed, and had to take to our oars. We rowed about two miles, and ran into a sand bar, and after we got well out of this trouble a heavy head wind arose, and the strong current of the river was against us. Dark night came on, and threatening rain. Every now and then we saw the lightning in the eastern horizon, and heard heavy peals of thunder. Thus we had a hard time before us, pulling against the current and wind, and hunting our way along the shore. But by perseverance we finally reached Kamloop by 11 o'clock at night.* Here is a large river steamer, which was built by the Hudson Bay Company during the gold excitement in 1865. It was built too large to be of practicable use either in the North or South Thompson Rivers. And further, the gold excitement soon died away, and the steamer was but of little use. Its engines are all taken apart, furniture stored away, and the boat is kept here awaiting better times or to decay. From Yale no boat can be brought up the Fraser to Lytton, nor is the Thompson navigable from Lytton to Kamloop Lake. What I said of the waters of the Fraser through the Fraser Canyon, is also applicable to the Thomspon from Lytton to the Lake.

The above steamer, the railroad survey were then using for their hotel, and when we arrived in the night we also took quarters in it, and without supper laid down on the floor of the boat and soon were asleep.

The night of the 13th of August was cold and rainy. This kind of weather is quite unexpected here. The oldest settlers say that they never saw so much rain at this season of the year. There is no doubt that if this part of the country had as frequent showers as they had the past few weeks, these hills, mountains and valleys would soon be covered with green verdure.

On the 14th, the railroad survey parties took their leave from Kamloop, Company Q. going up the North Thompson, and Company T. the South Thompson. The geological survey not

being ready, and thus having a little time, I will return and speak more fully of certain places, and of some of the views I was fortunate enough to obtain.

What I have seen of the country thus far is anything but desirable. When we enter the mouth of the Fraser River, the land as far as can be seen from the steamer is low, marshy and wet, thickly covered with swamp or sour grass for twenty or thirty miles up the river, and is, as I said, frequently flooded by the high tide. Thirty miles from the mouth of the Fraser, the land gradually rises, and begins to show more timber, and further up it is thickly covered with large pine trees, and is good timber land to within fifteen or twenty miles of Hope, or to the mouth of Harrison River. There, as I before said, we begin to enter the Cascade range, and as the mountains and rocks increase, the pines decrease. At Yale and through the Fraser Canyon the rocks and mountains predominate, and the pines are dwarfed and very few in number. Passing into the Northwestern side of the cascade range, we find sage brush growing abundantly, and also considerable bunch grass. The latter is very nutricious food for animals, and they thrive upon it very well, even if it is dried by the hot season.

From Lytton to Cook's Ferry there are high rugged mountains on each side of the Thompson River.* From Cook's Ferry to Savona Ferry, the country is principally barren, sandy, mountainous, hilly, and thickly covered with sage brush and bunch grass, and is upon the whole very uninviting.

A few attempts at farming have been made, and most of them, especially along the Fraser and up the Thompson as far as to within eight miles of Bonaparte River have been abandoned. A few farms are now in operation near Bonaparte, and between this and Kamloop with varied success. All the success depends

* Plate 29
* Plates 16 & 17

upon the facility they may have for irrigating the land. Without irrigation nothing would grow, and there seems to be but few places where it can practically be brought about.

Going on to a high hill in the rear of Kamloop, we have a beautiful view of the surrounding country.* Before me is the North Thomspon River and its valley running for many miles nearly directly from the north; on my right is the South Thompson River, up its valley one can see in a southwesterly direction for many miles. Below and a little to my right is the confluence of the two rivers in the foreground, along the north and east banks of which is the Kamloop Indian reserve, and still further back Mount St. Paul rises majestically.

At the foot of the hill is the Hudson's Bay Company's Station, – Kamloop, – composed of one dwelling, in which their agent, Mr. Jas. McKenzie, resides (latterly Mr. John Tait) – one store, two storage rooms, and the steamer of which I spoke, all of which belong to the Hudson's Bay Company. The united rivers – now the *Thompson* – flows steadily past, and off to my left, bestudded with islands, until it empties into Kamloop Lake. This lake has also many charms as seen from here, especially in the evening, when it reflects the beautiful rays of the setting sun. Its rugged shores, and sloping hills and mountains on either side, makes it a charming scene. Behind me are high hills and mountains, and united this scenery is very, *very* fascinating, and beautiful. Only one thing mars its beauty, and that is the barren appearance of these hills, mountains, and vallies. Only along the banks of the river can anything green be seen. A few desirable ranches or farms can also be seen along the river valleys, but all their verdure is produced by irrigation.

Now, a word or two with regard to the views I have taken which are not already described.

Hell's Gate, on the Thompson,* speaks for itself.

While I was at Tranquille Mills, viewing along the shore of the lake, I went up Tranquille River on to a high mountain terrace, about 800 feet above the sea level, and from there took a few views* of gravel columns and banks which are about 150 feet hivh. These are principally in the fore-ground of the pictures, while the back-ground is made up of mountains receding off toward the west, and these are thinly covered with bunch grass, wild sage, and dwarf pines.

Mr. George Watt, Commissary of the C.P.R.R. Survey, arrived at Kamloop on the morning of the 17th of August, and in a day or two after returned to Victoria. On the same day Mr. Selwyn suggested to Mr. Richardson that it would be advisable for him (Richardson) to leave our party and return to Bonaparte River, and go up the Cariboo road to Cariboo in a stage, and explore that region, and returning, explore the country along the road to Yale; then sail to Victoria and explore the coast of Vancouver's Island. Selwyn thought that this would be better, and more work would be accomplished than if we all stayed together and followed the same route. Mr. Richarson willingly entered into this arrangement, so we were deprived of his company the remainder of our journey. In the afternoon of the same day we took leave of Kamloop, took a regretful *good by* shaking of the hand with Mr. Richardson, and ferried our stores and baggage about a mile up the North Thompson River, and camped on a sand bank at the Indian Reserve. Here we had to wait a day or two to more properly organize our train. All the horses were brought, 15 in number – 12 packs and 3 riding horses. The men were all engaged, and our party for the expedition up the North Thompson River Valley now consisted of eight persons, namely:

A.R.C. Selwyn, Geologist.
B.F. Baltzly, Photographer.

* Plates 30 & 31
* Plate 18
* Plate 28

124

John Hammond, Asst. do.
John Peterson, Packer.
Philip Jago, (Indian) Asst. do.
James Dean, Cook.
Donald McPheal, Axeman and general Asst.
Abram La Rue, (Indian) Guide.

CHAPTER VI

Co. Q. of the R.R. Survey – Storm – Kamloop Indian Reserve – R.C. Mission Church – Lord's Prayer in Chinook – Indian Wigwams – Indian Winter Supplies – Departure from Kamloop – Dick – Trail to Clear Water – Red Pine Indian Reserve – Musquitos – Little Fort – Assinaboin Bluff – Clear Water

---

Since we are following the tracks of Co.Q. of the R.R. Survey, and often will be in their company, I might here give their strength. They have in all about 26 men, four pack trains, and a number of riding horses; altogether about 135 animals – making with ours about 150 horses and mules. They also brought 40 head of cattle for beef; these they drove along, and killed as they needed them.

At 4 p.m. of the day we left Kamloop a terrific storm passed over Kamloop Lake, over the mountains at Battle Bluff and up North Thompson Valley; however, we got but little of it at our camp. The view of the storm and lightning from here was grand – by far the finest I ever witnessed.

The Kamloop Indian Reserve, occupied by the Kamloop tribe, is about 2,000 acres in extent. The chief of this tribe is very sociable, and is the hardest worker among them. The tribe under this chief has adopted many of the improvements of civilization, excelling any I have ever yet seen. Most of them on this reserve live in houses of their own building, – principally log huts – clothe themselves more becomingly, and appear more intelligent than many others. A few of them have nice ranches on the reserve, and two of those are Philip and La Rue, our Indians.

The Catholics have laboured among them and gained a few proselytes. Their priest being away, they keep up their evening worship themselves, being led by the chief. They have a small log church, with mother earth for a floor and logs for seats. Outside, at the door fastening, is a small bell, fastened by a rope and at service the leader takes this bell and rings it before he opens the door and then enters, and the faithful follow and immediately begin their prayers by chanting and ringing of the bell. Their version of the Lord's Prayer is vastly different from the Scriptural. As it is strange and peculiar I will give it in the Chinook Jargon, or Indian trade language of the North Pacific Coast, and also a literal translation:

THE LORD'S PRAYER IN CHINOOK.

Nesika papa klaksta mitlite kopa saghalie, kloshe kopa nesika tumtum Mika nem; kloshe mika tyee kopa konaway tilikum; kloshe mika tumtum kopa illahie, kahkwa kopa saghalie. Potlatch konaway sun nesika muckamuck. Spose nesika mamook masahchie, wake mika hyas solleks, pe spose klaksta masahchie kopa nesika, wake nesika solleks kopa klaska. Mahsh siah kopa nesika konaway masahchie. KLOSHE KAHKWA.

TRANSLATION.

Our Father who stayeth in the above, good in our hearts (be) thy name; good thou chief among all people; good thy will upon earth as in the above. Give every day our food. If we do ill, (be) not thou very angry, and if any one evil towards us, not we angry towards them. Send away far from us all evil. GOOD SO.

Now, with regard to the other Indians I saw, the photograph taken of an Indian camp at Bonaparte will give a very good idea of their manner of living during the summer.* There it will be seen that a few have tents, or simply the fly of a tent drawn across a ridge pole, but I find the majority have only a few poles put up with cross pieces and the top slightly covered, some with rush matting of their make, and again others only with brush, while here and there we find a few poles standing against a tree with some brush over them. These are the wigwams of many of the present British Columbia Indians. Their winter wigwams are made in the earth. They dig a circular hole of about 25 to 30 feet in diameter and four feet deep; this they cover up – with the exception of a hole in the centre of about three feet in diameter – by placing heavy poles from the centre opening outwards, inclining like a roof, the end of the pole at the centre resting on strong uprights, and the other end on the earth. These poles are then covered with brush or limbs, and lastly with earth. The hole in the centre serves for ingress and egress; for light and the entrance of pure air, and the exit of foul air and smoke. In this cavern or wigwam there are often as many as a dozen families living during the winter.

The Indians at Victoria appear to be more civilized, but no more than those at Kamloop. Taking them upon an average they are a poor, miserable class of human beings, very immoral and depraved. The food of large numbers of them is dried salmon, – of which I spoke before – and 'olillie' (berry) cake. This is made of the sarves and other berries, bruised up and mixed with black moss, and then laid out flat and permitted to dry in the sun.

At 10 o'clock in the morning of the 19th of August, we left the camp at Kamloop Indian Reserve, and began our journey up the North Thompson. The horse allotted to me was a young black colt, only about three and a half years old, and quite wild, having been among the mountains free for some months, and needed breaking in. He, however, came very near *breaking me* in soon after we started. The girths of the saddle were not drawn tight enough, so after we had travelled about two miles he became restive, and began to *buck*, (jump and kick). The saddle bags flapped against his side, and frightened him the more, and in one of his plunges the saddle slipped to one side, and my only alternative was to leap off, which I did without injury. Away went the horse with the saddle under his feet. Mr. Selwyn being near by galloped after him; and now for a race: but after a half-mile run Selwyn caught him. I expected to find the saddle all torn to pieces, but, strange to say, it was all right except an unimportant rend. After adjusting the saddle, and taking the precaution to draw the girths tight this time, I got on again, and with a little care and kind treatment, got along very well. I named my horse 'Dick,' by which he will be known hereafter. By three p.m. we had travelled ten miles, and camped. Soon after it began to rain, and continued till ten in the evening. From this camp Mr. Selwyn and Hammond commenced pacing the trail and taking the bearings of the route. After resting over Sabbath we again moved camp, being the 21st of August. Sixteen miles from Kamloop we passed Mr. Knouff's ranch, which is the last farm in the North Thompson River Valley. He has a dairy, and makes some very desirable butter.

Part of the trail over which we travelled this day was very rough. Before we came to Knouff's ranch we passed along the side of a very steep bluff, and on our left the river was many hundred feet below us, while on the right the mountain rises a few thousand feet above us. At this bluff the railroad survey lost one of their horses and his cargo, which by some mis-

* Plates 19 & 20

hap fell over the precipice into the river. A few days after he was picked up at the Indian Reserve at Kamloop by the Indians. The cargo, consisting of ham and beans, they appropriated to themselves, as well as the horse, which they ate.

After travelling twelve and a half miles we camped in a beautiful little meadow. The next day we travelled twelve miles, and camped at the confluence of Lewis Creek and the North Thompson River. The trail was very rough, except some four miles, the greater part of it leading along the side of a very steep, rocky mountain, and at places there was scarcely foot-hold for the horses; but all went through safe. It is surprising to see how careful the horses and mules are in selecting footing in these dangerous paths. Thus far the country is slowly increasing in verdure, but, with the exception of a couple thousand acres of bottom land along the river, the mountains rise on each side higher and higher. The pines also become taller and more numerous.

After pitching our tents this evening, Mr. Selwyn and I tried to catch a few fish, but the musquitoes were more numerous than the fishes, and compelled us to make a hasty retreat.

On the 23rd of August we travelled 12 miles over a pretty good tract, and camped at the north end of the Red Pine Indian Reserve.[17] This is a small prairie of about 1,000 acres, forty-six and a half miles from Kamloop. The Catholics have also been here among the Indians; for I see in the centre of the plain a large wooden cross, a little log church, and one or two other small huts. Along the mountain are other wigwams, and here at our camp is a large log hut built some years ago by a Mr. Fortune; but all of which are now deserted. All the Indians and even cattle had to forsake this rich grassy prairie; and why? The cause evidently is the mosquitoe. We have been fearfully

troubled with them the past few days, and often we could scarcely eat our meals. We covered our necks and ears, and then ate with one hand, while with the other we tried to keep the persistent little pests away with our handkerchiefs; but with all this they would get to our hands and faces. They were about us like a swarm of bees and all trying to get a taste of our blood. Fortunately we had tents which were *mosquitoe tight,* in which we retired early in the evening, closed them up, and then at the little plagues which were unfortunate enough to be inside, and killed a couple hundred until they were all *cleaned* out, and then, oh! how we enjoyed the peace within, while without, the tent was perfectly covered with them trying to force their way in, and such a buzz and hum; it was frightful music. This, some may think is greatly exaggerated, but no; the description is not equal to the reality. I pitied the poor horses, and on the way I brushed them off my horse's neck and head, and thus tried to keep them away from him. This evening after he was turned loose he remembered my kindness, and followed me nearly every place. In spite of the musquitoes I took a view of the Reserve.*

The next day we travelled 10½ miles through swamps, thickets, across small prairies, and a steep bench or terrace of a mountain about 900 feet high, and camped at Little Fort, fifty-seven miles from Kamloop. On the mountain near us is an Indian camp. The chief is very talkative, and they seem to belong to Red Pine Reserve. Formerly, and even lately the Hudson's Bay Company used to send an agent during the winter to this place with some goods to trade with these Indians for furs. The following day we travelled 8 miles. Five miles from Little Fort we came to Assinaboine Bluff,* which rises abruptly from the water of the river. A zigzag track leads along its rugged side, the highest point of which is about 1,000 feet above the river. Below and above this are

* Plate 32
* Plate 33
17 Probably the North Thompson Indian Reserve.

vast boulders of rock, with here and there small ledges on which the hardy pine finds its foothold. The distance along the shore around the Bluff is only about 400 yards, while the trail along the Bluff is three-fourths of a mile. No laden train of either horse or mule can be taken across in safety, so we sent one of our party back to the Indian camp and hired a couple of Indians with a canoe to ferry our cargo around the Bluff, while others unpacked the train and took the horses across. Between Little Fort and this Bluff is an intensely thick forest of cedar and poplar trees, many of which are very large. This forest is in a bottom some three miles long and I think about a mile wide, and part of it is thickly covered with underbrush: Through this bottom or forest the trail passes, over fallen timber, across small mountain streams and swampy ground. After we got around the Bluff we started on, and travelling about two hours we saw a heavy storm arising and there was no possibility for us to camp, so we hastened on about a mile and came to an open flat. Just as we got there it began to rain a little, but the greater part of the storm passed north of us.

On Saturday, the 25th of August, we traveled across fallen timber, up and down steep banks and hills, through brush and trees, along rocky banks, etc., for a distance of 11 miles, and came to the crossing of the North Thompson, one mile above Clear Water. This day I went in advance of the party, and was fortunate in shooting several grouse. Although my little horse – Dick – *bucked* me off at the start, he is now as gentle and kind as any horse could be; and in shooting grouse [I] found no trouble in remaining on him, as he shied but very little at the report of a gun. Being in advance, I arrived at the crossing two hours before the train came up. Here I overtook Mr. McLennan and Q. party of the R.R. Survey. But before our train arrived they had left to go eight miles further up the river where they expected to camp for

the Sabbath. This was well, for grazing is not good here, especially for such a large number of animals. After the train arrived we took our cargo across the river in canoes (a couple of Indians happening to be here), and swam the horses over, pitched our tents, and soon after it began to rain.

Clear Water is rightly named. It is a beautiful stream about 200 or 300 feet wide and very rapid near its confluence with the North Thompson, which is seventy miles above Kamloop. I am told that some five or six miles above this stream are beautiful cascades, but which we could not visit.

It is now just two months since we left home, and in this time we have travelled by cars, boat, stage, on foot and horse 4,754 miles. Saw scenes and sights which I never expected to fall to my lot to witness. Received impressions which I know will never be forgotten.

CHAPTER VII

Raft River Cascade – North Thompson Valley above Raft River – Mad River – Sudden Halt – The Trail across the Mountain – Selwyn Lake – Selkirk Mountains – Difficulty of Trail Cutting – Descending the Mountain

---

The Gazette, July 8, 1872

On Monday, August 28th, we travelled to Raft River, distance seven miles from Clear Water. On the way coming, I saw, as we neared the river, a rocky opening in the mountains on my left, about a mile from the trail. After concluding to camp, I rode to the place through brush, over logs and rocks, etc., to view the cascade photographically. Here Raft River has cut its channel through mountains and rocks in ages past, and now rushes through them in a succession of falls and rapids.* The scenery, I think, is very fine; so I hurried back, and Mr. Hammond, Philip, LaRue and I hastily ate a little damper, drank some tea, and started with our *photo. horse*. We had to ford the river and cut part of the trail in order to get to the best view, but the scene richly repaid us for our trouble.

August 29th, we travelled 13 miles over a pretty good trail, and in the evening I took a beautiful view of the Great Bend of the North Thompson River. The next day we travelled nine miles, Hammond and I pacing for Selwyn.[18] Part of the trail was very rough, especially the last half. On each side are thickly wooded mountains 4000 or 5000 feet high, and in many places their steep sides descend to the river. The flats are few and small, not more than a fourth of a mile wide, and from half a mile to a mile in length. In passing through a small cedar swamp our photo. horse came very near to grief in a bog; but after some help he got out all right.

We are now evidently out of the mosquitoe region; for since we passed Clear Water we have not been troubled with them. We find blueberries in abundance here on the mountain terraces.

The following day (August 31st) after travelling one and a half miles we came to Mad River, a mountain stream of considerable size, 105½ miles from Kamloop.* The stream is full of boulders, and its waters rush through the mountains in continuous rapids. After travelling seven miles we caught up with the R.R. Survey party, who were camped in a small paddock 111 miles from Kamloop. Here the R.R. Survey and Mr. Selwyn held a consultation as to which course to take. The Indians said that there was no possibility for us to go along the river, for at Murchison's rapids, not far above this, there are many impassable bluffs, and there is no grazing for the horses above this

point. They said that the only way was for us to return to Mad River and go up the mountain and follow the water-shed of the mountains and thus cross over to Blue River near its confluence with the North Thompson. After duly considering the matter they decided to return and take the mountain trail. So on September 1st we retraced our steps to Mad River, recrossed and ascended the mountain about 1½ miles; altitude from the river 1600 feet.[19] Here we found on a terrace of the mountain a small swamp where we could obtain water, and therefore camped in connection with Co.Q party of the R.R. Survey. This camp is 107 miles from Kamloop. (In future I shall call Co.Q. of the R.R. Survey, *McLennan's party or men.*)

The trail up the mountain is very difficult to clear, or cut, as is seen from the fact that the next day, all of our and McLennan's axe-men were only able to cut about three and a half miles, so none of the trains left camp that day.

It appears that this mountain over which we have to pass is about 6,000 feet high, and the trail up its side passes through a thick forest of pine trees, which is full of fallen timber.

On Sept. 4th, after a rainy night we had a pleasant day, and at 1 p.m. left camp and began to ascend the mountain. The trail up the mountain is not so steep, but in many places very boggy. Its side is full of springs, and around those, and wherever there is a flattish place or terrace, it is boggy and wet. The highest point we reached to-day was 5,900 feet above the level of the sea, and at the summit we were greeted by a small lakelet covering about eight acres of ground. After travelling seven miles we camped at a small fen, surrounded with low white pine and balsam trees.

The trail over which we passed the next day was in many places almost impassable on account of the boggy nature of the soil on the ridge of these mountains. About four miles from our last camp we passed another small

* Plate 34
* Plate 35
18 Selwyn says 9¾ miles. Selwyn, 'Journal and Report,' 28.
19 Selwyn says 1150 feet. Ibid, 29.

lake covering about ten acres. It is about 400 feet lower than the summit, so it is about 5,500 feet above the sea. We travelled 7¾ miles, and descended 900 feet, and camped near a small brook. In this brook Hammond prospected for gold, but did not find even a trace of 'color.' Afterward Donald made a prospect only with a shovel, and soon after showed me about 40 cents worth of gold dust, and gave it to me to give to Selwyn. I did so, but upon further inquiry we found that Donald had gold dust with him, and we felt convinced that some it it, *accidentally*, got into the shovel, no doubt for a 'sell.' In passing along on the mountain top we frequently could see through openings in the low pine forest, the Selkirk range of mountains. They are in many places clad with snow, and here and there large glaciers can distinctly be seen. Upon the whole they appear quite rugged and grand.

On Sept. 6th, in the afternoon, we travelled six miles over a far better trail than what we had the day before, gradually rising until we struck a small boggy prairie valley, through which a nice stream of water passes, supposed either to be the head of Raft River or one of its tributaries. We went up this stream about a mile, and then crossed it and travelled westward, and arose gradually until we crossed the water-shed of this mountain and came to a few small lakes, supposed to be the head-waters of Mad River. These are a chain of three lakes surrounded with fens, interspersed with small pines, etc. We camped at the lower and smallest of the three lakelets (of which camp and lake I took a stereo view.)* We had considerable rain this day, although quite cold.

On the morning of the 7th Sept. the ground was covered with a stiff frost, and ice had formed during the night a quarter of an inch in thickness. We travelled 10½ miles, in which we descended the mountain 1000 feet, and found a great change in the temperature, although it kept pretty cold the whole day, and some snow fell.

This morning we passed the two lakes already mentioned, and I took a view of the upper one,* crossed the water-shed and came to another small lake, supposed to be the head of a tributary of Blue River. We passed down the outlet of this lake, through a forest, on over a large prairie, dryer than any we have had as yet, into the woods again, and up a boggy hill, on the top of which is a strange little lake. On one side of it is a kind of an embankment of soft turf or mud, covered with grass. Between this lake and a swamp on our left is a rocky path, over which the trail leads, then down a steep rocky hill, across another small swampy valley, up and along side of a very boggy mountain, where we passed McLennon's mule trains, many of them sticking in the mire. Thus we journeyed on till we came to a small fen and camped. The grazing here was very poor.

The next day we travelled three and a quarter miles over a pretty good trail, and finding very good pasture Selwyn thought it wise to halt and camp. This camping ground is exceedingly beautiful. A few rods below us is a small lake, bordered with prairie, interspersed with small clusters of pine and balsam trees. West of us rises a small hill from which, by looking eastward, a beautiful view of the snow-clad Selkirk mountains can be enjoyed,* by looking westward we see other snow ranges of rather imposing command running along far west of Blue River. In our travels to-day we gradually ascended until we are again 5750 feet above the sea. It was cold the whole day, and considerable ice formed. A high hill rises up before us northward from us, about half a mile distant, and on the 9th Selwyn, Hammond, and I went up on the top of it, and were well paid for our walk. The scene in a clear day must be grand and sublime. That day it was very gloomy, and a snowstorm was raging among the snow-clad

* Plates 36 & 37
* Plates 42 & 43
* Plates 38-41

mountains, and the atmosphere between them and us had a blue hazy or smoky appearance, and much of the beauty of the scenery was lost. Yet even then there was much here to admire. Nearly due west from this point is a large lake; I suppose it is about 15 miles away, and far beyond this are seen more snow-clad peaks. Evidently Blue River flows from this lake, and as it was discovered by Mr. Selwyn I suggest that it be named Selwyn Lake.[20] It is nestled under snow clad peaks, which are its never-failing sources. It seems to offer a surprising variety of charming scenery, in which the grassy slopes along its shores present a pleasing contrast to the grand and rugged aspect of the mountain range that surmount and over top it. Its circumference is indented with innumerable bays and harbours. In its peaceful moods, Selwyn Lake must be unsurpassed in quiet, dreamy beauty and romantic attractions. Sylvan and fairy-like glades, sparkling in the sunlight, blend with tracts of sober woodland. In imagination, no description can do justice to the moonlight effects on this lake when its surface, unruffled by the faintest breeze resembles molten silver, stretching away until lost in the shadows of the distant mountains.

Beside this lake we have other attractions which demand our attention. Looking southwest, east and north-east we have a grand view of the Selkirk mountain range with its bold bluffs, pinicles, boulders and chasms, much part of them being covered with perpetual snow. Here and there small mountain streems can be seen rushing down their sides, and appearing like silver threads. Large glaciers can also be seen lying in the deep mountain gorges. Beneath looking north-west we again see the North Thompson, and its valley, and as seen from here one would scarcely believe it to be the broad and rapid stream that it is. Those mountains, lakes, and rivers, as seen from this point of observation, has a tendency to raise our thoughts and feelings from the created to the Creator. How grand! how sublime! are all these wonders. But the greatness and majesty of the Creator words cannot express, nor mind comprehend.

Our train only moved 1½ miles on this day, the trail not being cut any further. The trees along the mountain ridge show evidence that the snow in the winter is very deep; the branches principally hang downwards, no doubt caused by the weight of the snow and ice.

On the morning of Sept. 12th, we bid adieu to the camp of the 9th, and began to descend the mountains, the sides of which are in many places very steep. The mountain rises at an angle of from 30 to 40 degrees, down which this trail twists in a zigzag course. Frequently it is broken by terraces or flats on the mountain side, where are small lakes of beautiful cold clear water. After descending, we again came to the North Thompson River with its muddy water. But soon the trail rises again several hundred feet to cross a thickly wooded ridge, which extends up to the river's edge, leaving no room for the trail. After crossing this ridge, we came to a small stream running from the west. This stream had to be bridged, by felling three large trees across it and placing them together with a few benches in the centre to support them. Our train crossed safely, but one of McLennan's mules getting one of his hind feet between the logs, fell and broke his leg. In coming down the mountain one of our horses fell and rolled over three or four times, but was stopped by coming in contact with a tree. It is of a frequent occurrence to see some of McLennan's horses and mules down in a bog, or rolling down a hill or mountain side, and sometimes laying with packs down and heels up. We camped this evening on the bank of the North Thompson River, near the above stream. Here is pretty good grazing for our horses, but a miserable place for camping. In coming down

20 Probably present day Murtle Lake.

131

from this mountain – descending 3,750 feet – we travelled eight and a half miles, making the distance from Kamloop 151½ miles to our camp, which we called 'Wild Goose Camp,' for here we saw the first wild goose on our journey. It is not strange that our men do not make better progress in cutting a trail through these cedar forests. Milton and Dr. Cheadle speak the truth when they say, in speaking of this place. 'The fallen trees lay piled around, forming barriers often six or eight feet high on every side; trunks of huge cedars, moss-grown and decayed, lay half buried in the ground on which others as mighty had recently fallen, trees still green and living, recently blown down, blocking the view with the walls of earth held in their matted roots; living trunks, dead trunks, rotten trunks, dry barkless trunks, and trunks moist and green with moss; bare trunks, and trunks with branches – prostrate, reclining, horizontal, proped up at different angles, timber of every size, in every stage of growth and decay, in every possible position, entangled in every possible combination.'[21] Much of the swampy ground is densely covered with thickets of the aralea, a tough-stemmed trailer, with leaves as large as the rhubarb plant, and growing in many places as high as our shoulders. Both stems and leaves are covered with sharp spines, and make it very unpleasant for the axe-men to to cut the trail.

CHAPTER VIII

Wild Goose Camp – An Emigrant's Grave – Short Supplies – Blue River – Muddy River – Kitty – Grouse Stew – The First Canoe – Canoe Camp – Indian Hunter and his Klootshman – Views – Cedar Forests

At 'Wild Goose Camp' we had to remain for several days waiting for the trail to be cut. Part of this time the sky was darkened with a dense smoke, caused, no doubt, by the woods being on fire.

Here at our camp we have to be very careful, in order not to fire the woods. The ground is full of vegetable matter to the depth of about 8 inches. When this is dry it burns very rapidly, and at times, when we think our camp fires all put out, we find them a few hours after starting up from under the moss, several feet from the camp fire, and burning with a fearful heat.

Looking through the smoky atmosphere, toward the east, we can faintly trace the outlines of a high peak, rising high above, and lying far beyond the river range of mountains.

A little to the right of this is a deep gorge, through which flows a large stream of water over continuous falls and rapids. At the confluence of this with the North Thompson River, the latter makes a great bend, as if to meet this mountain stream. I went to the extreme end of this *bend,* to see whether I could obtain a view of the falls. The distance was about half a mile through the worst wood I ever saw. Logs piled on each other, brush in every possible position, the aralea, wild gooseberry bushes, etc., obstructed my passage so much that I at one time was tempted to return to camp. However, I persevered, and although I did not find the view of the falls worthy of a

21 Viscount Milton & W.B. Cheadle, *The North-West Passage by Land* (London: Cassell, Petter & Galpin, 1865), 287.

photo, yet I was not sorry for having made the trip.

At the extreme end of the bend, immediately opposite the confluence of the above stream, by the side of a large cedar tree, I came across a whiteman's grave. It appears that here is buried one of the sixty Canadian emigrants, who crossed through the Rocky Mountains, at Leather Pass, for British Columbia in 1862.[22] Sad reflections arose in my mind while standing beside the grave. Here alone, far away from home or friends, *alone,* in the wilderness of the North Thompson Valley he lies to moulder and decay. Here *alone,* and perhaps already forgotten, as no tombstone marks the spot; only a rough head-board, which is already fast disappearing, and in a few years the spot will be so covered with grass, moss and fallen timber that the grave will be among the things of the past. But such is our life. To-day we live; in a few years we die and are soon forgotten, even by our dearest friends here. But, thanks be to God, we have a higher hope. Although these bodies decay and moulder to the dust, yet there is again a reunion of soul and body; a joyful reunion around the throne of God. To a Christian this dark picture of the grave brightens to one of glory, as we look upon Christ, our elder brother, who also descended into the grave, but soon burst asunder its bars, arose and is now sitting on the right hand of the Father. In Him we have hope. A blessed hope of immortality; a hope of a reunion with these bodies, long forgotten. A reunion with our dear friends who have gone before us, and those who shall follow after us; and still better, a hope to live with Him who redeemed us. Oh! what a precious *hope* this is.

A little above this grave I found the remains of a carpet sack, no doubt once the property of him who lies in yonder grave. Still further up the river, I found an Indian fishing net in pretty good condition, entangled amongst some bushes at the waters edge. It, I suppose, got washed away from its owner, far above, in the late high water. Here, also, I see marks of the trail cut, do doubt, by Lord Milton and Dr. Cheadle in 1863.

Our 'Wild Goose Camp,' I have no hesitancy in saying, is in the same locality where Milton and Cheadle ran short of provisions and had to kill one of their horses; and this happening to be a black one they called it *Black Horse Camp.*

The timber here is very large – I measured a cedar tree which was 22 feet in circumference.

Another reason, aside from what I already stated, why these woods are easily fired, and why the fires rage so fearfully in these forests, is – the bark, sapwood, leaves and twigs of these pines, fir, balsam, and hemlock trees are well saturated with resinious substance, therefore, the whole of the woods are highly inflamable. The rainy season seems to have fairly set in; for nearly the whole time we were at this camp, we had rain.

At my suggestion, Mr. Selwyn placed upon me the commissary department of our party, thus giving him more time to attend to his Geological work. I am, therefore, after this, *Commissary* as well as photographer of the party. Selwyn only bought two months provisions, thinking that he would not be longer than that in the mountains. He had no idea of the difficulties he had to encounter. Already we had been in the mountains five weeks, and had made only about one-third of our journey to the Jasper House, on the east side of the Rocky Mountains. Some part of our provisions were already getting short, and we had not more than half enough sugar and beans. The former was already all used up, except 14 pounds, and other things had gone in a kind of haphazard way. The cook and others had access to the cargo at will, and things went faster than they should. Therefore, my suggestion to the necessity of having a commissary. Upon taking this

22 i.e. Yellowhead Pass.

133

department I took an inventory of what we had left, and put the party on short allowance, cutting off one pound per day from each man. Our week's allowance for our party of eight was now –

70 lbs. flour, 70 lbs. bacon, 9 lbs. beans, 3 lbs. rice, 2 boxes yeast powders, 1 oz. pepper, 4 lbs. dried apples, 2 lbs. sugar, 1¾ lbs. tea, 5 lbs. oatmeal, 1 lb. coffee, 1 lb. salt, 1 qrt. bottle pickles, 9 candles, 2 lbs. soap.

The above allowance gives three pounds – all told – to each man per day; the regular allowance being *four* pounds. We needed more of certain articles – for instance beans and sugar – but as long as flour and bacon lasted we felt that we would not starve.

On Monday, Sept. 18th, we left 'Wild Goose Camp,' and traveled 6¼ miles, and camped near a large marsh covered with swamp grass. Two and a half miles from the former camp we crossed Blue River, which flows from the west and empties into the North Thompson River. About a mile further up we passed the mouth of Muddy River,[23] flowing through the mountains from the east, and also emptying into the North Thompson. The waters of Muddy River are principally glacier – at least so Mr. Selwyn thinks – and consequently are very, very muddy, and the stream is rightly named. The water rushing through the streets of Montreal during a heavy rain-storm will give a correct idea of the water of this river. The waters of the North Thompson above its confluence with Muddy, is, comparatively speaking, quite clear, and for about two miles below, the waters of the two streams flow together side by side unmixed, showing a strange contrast.

Two miles above this, by looking back, we see near the above confluence two mountain peaks about 9000 feet high. In the gorge between them is a small glacier, and the scene is peculiarly beautiful.

On the next day we were again waiting for the trail. I overhauled some of the cargo, and after doing up a *washing*-and-IRONING, I went out hunting. I forgot to mention quite an important personage in our party, and that is a little dog – Kitty. To her did we owe many a good dish of grouse; and indeed were it not for her we would very seldom have fared this luxury. In my hunt Kitty accompanied me, and in about two hours we returned with half a dozen large grouse. Philip and I prepared them, and I done the cooking myself, rather than permit our greasy cook to spoil them for us. Every one seemed to enjoy the dish of grouse stew immensely, and I think I did as much as any one, for I knew that it was *clean*. This much could not be said at all times with regard to the dishes set before us by our cook. Often it was best for us to eat without asking questions. I am certain the cook was a 'fish out of water;' a *man* in the wrong place. The past two days it was quite warm, but the nights very cold and heavy frost.

On the 20th of September we travelled eight miles. The greater part of the way the trail was pretty good, but a little boggy in places. The cedar trees, and also hemlock, are very large along the route, and the ground in many places is completely covered with the ever-detested aralea.

The North Thompson, as far as we travelled to-day, and, I am informed, for some distance up the river, is thickly bestuded with small islands. At our last camp a few of McLennan's men made a canoe. One of them and our LaRue started up the river with it this morning; but it was not made according to 'Gunther', and therefore was not a 'sea going' vessel, and had to be abandoned after a four miles paddling. A short time before we camped this evening we crossed a rapid, rocky, and nameless river of clear water, about 100 yards wide, and quite shallow. There was a drizzly rain the whole day, and just as we began to camp the

23 Probably modern-day Mud Creek.

rain began to pour down, and in this we had the *pleasure* of pitching our tents; the packers to unpack their horses, and the cook prepare supper. Here, evidently, is the place where Milton says he found the first grass for ten days. The locality corresponds exactly to his description of his travels on the 3rd of August, 1863. Here, or within sixty rods of our camp, is the marsh of about 300 yards in length; below is the river, which they crossed in the evening of the same day.

Here we were again in a mighty cedar forest, filled up with brush and thickets of every description, and consequently waiting for the trail. Hammond and I put in part of this time tailoring, cobblering, washing, etc. A few of McLennan's men, and two of ours, built another canoe here, under the guidance of LaRue, hence we call this 'Canoe Camp,' 165³/₄ miles from Kamloop. We had almost continual rain until the morning of the 22nd, when the clouds broke away for a time and disclosed to us the tops of the mountains again. The snow was laying lower on the side of the mountains, and this admonished us that ere long we would have snow here also in abundance. About noon we saw an Indian and his squaw paddling down the river in a canoe. We hailed them, and they came to shore and gave us some valuable information (LaRue being our translator). This Indian and his *klootshman* (squaw) are out among these mountains hunting, and according to their account were quite successful. They say that they killed 6 grizzly bears, 13 black or brown bears, 28 beavers etc., during the past three months. How these Indians endure the rain and cold is a marvel to me. This one has nothing on him but a torn buckskin shirt and a piece of a dirty blanket over his shoulders. His *klootshman* had evidently nothing on, or over her but a single green blanket, and they had nothing on their heads, feet or limbs. Night and day this appears to be all they have. In my

visits to some of their wigwams, a hundred miles below, I found them just as above described. A few fare better but they are rather the exception, especially among these mountain Indian hunters. Here there are no Indian camps, these two, and others hunting have their homes many miles from here. This afternoon one of McLennan's trains came in, and close to our camp, near the bank of the river, one of their horses bogged and fell on the edge of the bank. After his packs were loosened he made an effort to get up, but in doing so he fell over the bank into the river. There he would have drowned, or died at the water's edge – for he made but few very feeble attempts to get out – were it not that a number of us cut a way down and pulled him on to the bank, and then raised him up. The poor fellow was almost stiff with cold. The feed which the horses and mules had for the previous few weeks was very poor in quality, although, generally, plenty in quantity, – and they were rapidly loosing strength. The grass is principally found in marshes and is therefore swamp or sour grass, and this affords but very little nourishment.

I took several views here, one view of some snow clad mountains on the east side of the river.* Another showing the huge cedar trees, or rather cedar forests in this locality,* and still another of 'Canoe Camp' after a stormy night.* The last shows how we live in the woods, while the second gives a correct idea of the density of the forests and of the difficulty of trail cutting here. As a forest the scenery is beautiful. The trees grow very close together, and the trunks are from a foot to nine feet in diameter and many rise in almost perfect perpendicularity for hundreds of feet and with little or no diminution of size more than a hundred feet without limb. Others equally giant-like, crooked and gnarled, aid to make the forest picturesque. And while all is perfect stillness and rest and shadow on the ground, we, look-

* Plate 44
* Plate 45
* Plate 46

ing to where the sky is perceptible here and there through the thick foliage, can see the flexible tops swinging from side to side in the roaring mountain breeze. The soil, being never visited by the sun, is always moist, and produce a luxuriant and beautiful undergrowth of ferns, mosses, shrubs and plants, including our enemy the aralea. When in these forests, I at times compared myself to a merman, who while at the bottom of the ocean, amid a large growth of queer sea-weed, and surrounded by beautiful shells and the treasurer of a thousand wrecks, should look up from his abo[d]e of peace, and see the surface of the water f[a]r above him, raging in a terrific storm.

CHAPTER IX

Horses Failing – Limestone River – Snow Clad Peaks and Glaciers – Slow Travelling – Mount Cheadle – Garnet River Cascade – Photographing the Cascade and Mount Cheadle – Canadian Emigrants – 'Slaughter Camp' – Forts of the North Thompson River – Horse Lost – Emigrant Trail – More Mountain Peaks and Glaciers – Beaver Creek

---

The Gazette, July 25, 1872

The canoe being finished LaRue and one of McLellan's[24] men started up the river with it to follow the R.R. Survey kitchen train.

On the 25th of Sept. we left 'Canoe Camp,' – after being there for five days waiting for the trail to be opened, and during the whole of this time we had rain except a few hours on the 23rd. In six and a half hours of hard travel we only travelled 7 miles, the trail being very rough, and rain the whole day. The horses were daily getting weaker for want of proper food, and although their packs were getting lighter daily, yet their strength decreased more rapidly than the weight of their packages. After travelling about three miles we crossed a large rapid, rocky stream flowing into the Thompson from the West, which Selwyn christened *Limestone River.*[25] A little above this river on the east side of the North Thompson are a couple of beautiful snow-clad peaks, between which is a glacier of considerable size. The green blocks of ice could plainly be seen from the trail, but the rain prevented me from obtaining a view. The next day we were again waiting for the opening of the trail, and it was the first pleasant day we had for some time. During the past month we only travelled 97 miles; this is an average of only 3¾ miles per day. The forest is so dense, and the undergrowth so thickly filled up with the aralea, alder and tall cranberry trees, and fallen timber of every description, that it is impossible to make more than from one to four miles of trail per day. This, and the near approach of snow, and the small amount of provisions on hand, made our journey begin to look gloomy.

Sept. 27th, 11 a.m. – The weather looked very gloomy, and while we were preparing to move camp a heavy storm was raging on the top of the mountains before us; but at camp we had no rain as yet. It was a grand sight to see the clouds and rain chased and driven about on the mountain top by the wind, while we were in almost a perfect calm. However, this was of a short duration, for an hour after we got rain in torrents. We travelled 4½ miles over a pretty good trail; passed Mount Cheadle, which is on the east side of the North Thompson River, 176 miles above Kamloop.* The mountain is about 8,000 feet high, and is heavily timbered from its base to within a few thousand feet of its summit. A little above this, through a large gorge, we saw a considerable stream flowing into the Thompson from the east. As it rushes through

* Plate 47
24 i.e. McLennan.
25 Probably present day Miledge Creek.

this chasm, it forms a grand cascade, and is indeed very beautiful as seen from the trail on the west side of the river.

Our camp this evening was the most pleasant we have had for a long time. Our tent was under a very large hemlock tree close to the river. As I said the limbs of those and other trees among these mountain ranges are all hanging downwards, and thus shedding the rain and leaving the ground perfectly dry around them for about eight or ten feet.

Another halt for the trail; so the next morning there being some signs of clearing up, I was highly elated with the prospect of getting a few views of Mount Cheadle and the cascade. Thinking the land opposite our camp was the mainland, I got LaRue to take me across in the canoe. Then I started through the willow, alder, and t[a]ll-cranberry trees and ferns, wet with the last night's rain, to go to the cascade to see whether there was any prospect of getting views near the falls. After plodding on about three-fourths of a mile through the above bushes, across bear tracks (one evidently very large judging from the marks of his claws), shooting a grouse, and passing an old deserted Indian hunter's camp and cabin, I found, by coming to a slue or arm of the river, that I was only on a large island. So I returned, deeply chagrined, and when I got opposite the camp, Hammond and LaRue came over with the canoe. I told them my mistake, and also that I was determined to go to the falls, this time with the canoe; so away we went down stream. The river flows very rapidly, thus without much paddling it only took us twenty-five minutes to reach the cascade. The cascade, as seen from the foot of the falls, is grand beyond conception.* It is by far the boldest scenery of the kind I ever witnessed. It made my heart throb with wonder and amazement as I stood for a few moments and looked upon this beautiful sheet of water as it dashes and tumbles down over the rocks with a deep thundering and roaring noise. The height of the falls is altogether about 400 feet. Far above it runs down a narrow canyon in angry, foaming sheets, and then makes a bold leap over a perpendicular rock for many feet down, and dashes against a rock which turns its course a little to the right; again it makes another fearful leap, but is again arrested by another rock which has a front of about 200 feet. Here the water separates, the most part running over a rocky precipice on the right, and on the left the water flows down over the brow in thin sheets, to a distance of 150 feet, and before it reaches the rocks beneath it breaks into a shower of spray, and looks much like a white veil against the dark rocks over which it flows. In the centre the rocks boldly project, and only here and there small streams of water flow over them, looking much like silver threads. The velocity of the falling waters keeps up a continuous hurricane at the brow and foot of the falls, and for many yards around the foliage and trees are kept in continual motion with the wind, and wet with the spray. We did not stay long to admire its beauties, but hastened back to our canoe to return to camp for our instruments; but when we reached camp it began to rain. The current was so strong that it took us an hour and a half to get back, and from paddling, pushing, and towing the canoe against the current we got a complete drenching.

The following day being a little more pleasant, Hammond, LaRue and I, accompanied by Selwyn, started for the cascade again. Not being able to get near the falls with the canoe, we cut about 40 rods of trail, and carried our instruments near the foot of the falls. After Selwyn took a look at the cascade, and examined the rocks, etc., he left us, Hammond and LaRue taking him across the River Thompson to our trail on the west bank. The day was very cloudy and gloomy, yet I was successful in get-

* Plates 48 & 49

137

ting a few good views. The upper rapids we could not get in our view, it being hid by the dense forests of dark green pine and balsam trees. Mr. Selwyn named the stream 'Garnet River,' and therefore the falls 'Garnet Cascade.'[26]

After taking the above view we carried our instruments back to the canoe, and went up the Thompson about half a mile and stopped on the west bank of the river (trail side). Here we carried our instruments up a high bank about 200 feet, and then along the trail for a quarter of a mile, to a point where a good view of Mount Cheadle could be obtained. After taking a view of the Mount we repacked the instruments and left them in the woods for the night, thinking it not safe to take them up to camp in the canoe, preferring to bring them the next day on a pack horse. The feed of our poor horses is very poor; they having but little more than leaves and twigs.

On Oct. 1, we again got on the way, travelled five miles and camped on a rocky bank near the river. After travelling about three miles, we passed the sixty Canadian emigrants' 'Slaughter Camp.' Ten years ago a large number of men left their Canadian homes, and turned their faces westward to find homes in British Columbia, or perhaps more properly at the Cariboo gold diggings. They passed Edmonton, and Jasper House on the east of the Rocky Mountains, and on through Leather Pass to Tete Juan Cache[27] on the western side. Thus far they overcame every difficulty, but at Tete Juan Cache the company divided, part going down the Fraser, – of these I could learn but little, – while the other part, consisting of 60 men, turned southward, passed Cranberry Lake, crossed Canoe River, and journeyed on to Albredy Lake, and finally came to the North Thompson Forks. After vainly endeavoring to cut their way to Cariboo, up the north-west branch of the North Thompson, they turned

their course south in order to reach Kamloop by following the North Thompson River. In a few days their provisions gave out, and they found the steep sides of the mountains and bluffs extend to the water's edge, and the forest so thick that their progress was so slow and difficult that they gave up in despair the design of making their way by land. So here they killed all their cattle and dried the beef. (Thus the name 'Slaughter Camp'). They deserted 40 or 50 horses, threw away their pack saddles, built canoes and rafts, and entrusted themselves to the dangers of an unknown river – the North Thompson. 'All went well with the voyagers until they reached Murchison's, or Grand Rapids. The men on the leading rafts did not perceive the danger until too late to avoid it, and the rafts were sucked into the rapids in spite of all their efforts, and many of the unfortunate people were drowned. Those who followed were warned in time by the fate of their companions and succeeded in reaching the shore in safety. They had now to cut their way along the precipitous banks. After reaching the lower end of Murchison's Rapids they again made rafts, and shooting the lower rapids safely, arrived in wretched plight at Kamloop.'

Here – Slaughter Camp – remains of their saddles are still lying about, and for some distance we can see where they cut large cedars for their rafts. Here and there we can see places where they built canoes, and at one place we found an inscription on a tree, viz.: 'Slaughter Camp, Aug. 5th 1862, Kemps, Whitley, Miller.'

The next day we travelled four miles and came to the Forks of the North Thompson. At the confluence of the two branches, the west branch has several islands. In order to avoid bridging and crossing so many arms of the stream Mr. McLennan thought it would be better to cross the river above the islands. About

26 Probably present day Pyramid Creek. On the photographs Garnet River is referred to as Hammond River.

27 i.e. Tête Jaune Cache. Baltzly adheres to this mistaken spelling throughout.

half a mile back there were two trails blazed by the emigrants. The one we took led us to the Forks, so we turned on to this trail, cut the trail up this stream with the hope of reaching Cariboo; but coming to this bluff, became discouraged, and turned their course, as I said, for Kamloop.[28] After consulting whether it would be best to cross west branch here and cut our way down the other side to the Emigrants trail or return and cross at the islands, we decided to do the latter. So on the 3rd of October we returned to the Forks; but after arriving the parties determined to cross the main river, and go up the east bank and cross the north branch over to the emigrant trail. We had almost continual rain, and betimes heavy showers during this day, and the past three days the river rose three feet. The first night we were at this camp one of our horses died from cold and exhaustion, or rather from want of proper food.

In order to cross the river, and get our cargoes across properly, we had to make another canoe; this we lashed or tied with the one made at 'Canoe Camp,' and thus made a canoe raft. Here are a few rugged mountain peaks. When we first saw them they were entirely free from snow; but after a storm which raged only for half an hour, we saw, when the clouds cleared away, that they were well covered with snow. This was, indeed, a sudden transformation.

On the 5th of October our canoe raft was completed, and we soon had our cargoes across, and the horses swam the river. By noon we had the trains packed, and a quarter of a mile's travel brought us to the north branch, which we forded without any difficulty, and arrived at the emigrant trail and camp at the confluence of the two branches or forks of the Thompson, 186½ miles above Kamloop. Here an inscription on a tree tells us that the Indian guide of the emigrants – 'Andrew Cardinal' –

left them, and returned back to Edmonton, on the eastern side of the Rocky Mountains. We continued our course up the North Branch 1½ miles further and camped.

On the following day our horses could not all be found till late in the afternoon, and we, therefore, did not move camp. In searching for grass they got scattered, and for a time we feared that a few of them could not be found at all. A short distance from here, close to the river, is an Indian grave, from all appearance newly made. The man was evidently a convert to Catholicism, for at the head of the grave is a small wooden cross, upon which is tied a leaf from a prayer book, – the pictures of the Virgin Mary and the infant Christ. A few steps from this are the ruins of his camp, and a canoe; still a little further off, on a tree, are three beaver skins, and some dried meat, etc.; and thus is seen that, although he may have been a convert, yet he still held fast to the Indian customs. During the past night and this morning it rained, but by noon the clouds broke away, and revealed to us about as pretty mountain scenery, peaks, and glacier as I ever saw to be close sufficient to take an effective view. I think the peaks are about 9,000 feet high, and covered with perpetual snow. They are on the east of the North Branch. I was very lucky, indeed, to get a view here,* for almost immediately after my plates were exposed, the peaks were again covered with clouds and not seen again. It is wonderful, to see how the clouds hover and linger around these snow clad mountain peaks. Here McLennan's party killed one of their bullocks, and we obtained a portion of it. I requested the cook to make some rice soup, but soon saw that he knew but little about it, and I had to give him a lesson in cooking by 'practical demonstration.' LaRue said that the soup was 'hyas kloshe muck-amuck,' (very good food,) to this the whole party assented, if not by word, it was by the

* Plate 50
28 Evidently one or more lines were skipped when the type was set from Baltzly's original manuscript.

frequency that their plates were filled.

On the 7th of Oct., we travelled 5¾ miles, and we went along the west bank or side of the North Branch of the North Thompson River, crossed three streams flowing from the west and northwest. The last of these was turned from its channel by either floodwood or a beaver dam, (I am inclined to believe the latter) and it was making a new channel through the woods, rolling, and tumbling through brush, around trees, over and under logs, and here and there where the soil is loose it has already succeeded in cutting a channel. I named the stream Beaver Creek.* A short distance from this creek we ascended a very steep grade on to a high terrace of the mountain. Along this we traveled for about half a mile when we again descended a steeper grade to the river bank. Soon after we crossed the river to the east side, and followed the east bank about three-fourths of a mile and camped. A great deal of snow fell on the mountains this day. From the valley, we could see the snow flakes steadily falling without being driven by the wind. The effect was exactly like that produced by the stereoptigon [stereopticon] in a winter or snow scene, only upon a large and grander scale.

CHAPTER X

Selwyn and LaRue start in advance – Wretched Plight of the Pack Animals – Burnt Woods – Mount Milton – Blueberries – Albreda Lake – McLennan River – New Indian Guide – Arrival at Canoe River – Canoe and McLennan River Valleys – Selwyn and LaRue – Mountain Scenery at Canoe River – Trains and Men Ordered Back to Kamloop

On the 9th of Oct., at the suggestion of Mr. McLennan; Mr. Selwyn and LaRue took four days' provisions and started in advance to try if possible to get to Cranberry Lake and see whether Mr. Mahood, of Company R. of the C.P.R.R. survey, and his company, who went up to Cariboo, and were to work their way across to this lake – were successful in their undertaking or not; and if successful to assertain what kind of a trail there is across to Cariboo, and the distance, etc. Our movements depended much upon Mahood's success or failures. Near here I took a view of a water washed bank, where the trees were for some distance lying horizontal across the river, making it a very peculiar scene.* This day we traveled 4¼ miles, and the scenery was rather uninteresting. The trees in this valley are much smaller than at or below the Forks. This evening, Mr. McLennan read a letter to Hammond and me, which he had just received from Mr. Green, Chief of McLennan's or Q. party, and who is now at the Forks with the packers. One of his packers, Mr. Coonie, who went back from Blue River to clear water for another cargo, returned and caught up at the Forks. The statement Mr. Green gave of the matters among their packers made every thing look dark, *very dark* for them and us. One of their trains – Mr. Jamison's – had only fourteen horses left, which were able to carry packs, and these had to be light. Four of the horses were dead, and the rest were left behind either to die or to gather up strength if they could find feed. The mule train, under charge of a few Spaniards, had only seventeen able to carry light packs; of the others, some were dead, some abandoned to do the best they could, and a few walked along without packs. Mr. Coony's train had done the best; for as yet none of his mules died, and only two were left behind. All the others were able to pack and in pretty good condition. McLennan's kitchen train of 16 horses were about used up. It was fearful to look at many of these poor animals,

* Plate 52
* Plate 53

140

for their backs were covered with wounds and sores, caused by the packs, and the stench from some of them was almost unendurable. Some of the wounds were from 6 to 8 inches in diameter, and yet packs were put upon them. (The prevention of cruelty to animals, or law relating to it, was not in force.) This was the state of the pack trains, and it was really bad enough; but our position was still worse. All the packers wanted to return, ours included; Peterson said we had no business here in the mountains at this season of the year if we at all expected to get our animals back. Mr. Coony said that in crossing the mountain between Mad and Blue rivers he had to pass through eight inches of snow, and he feared that he would not be able to recross with his train even then, and his Indian assistants declined to go any further. Thus everything looked gloomy.

At the request of Mr. Selwyn I took charge of our company during his absence; so the next day I sent our train back to assist McLennan's train in bringing forward their cargo. My horse, (Dick) poor fellow was getting very weak, although I had not ridden him for the previous three or four weeks.

On Oct. 11th, after a cold rainy night, we got again on the way, and travelled 9 miles. Soon after we left camp we came to burnt timber.* This whole tract of land was burnt apparently at different periods. Four miles from last night's camp we came to a very stony mountain, along the side of which the trail led. Looking south-east from this point we saw a few rugged peaks with a large glacier between them. The centre and immediately back of this glacier was covered with clouds, and what lay beyond was not revealed until the morning of the next day before sun rise, when we saw immediately beyond the glacier a bold conical peak rising majestically thousands of feet above the others, and at the rising of the sun [it] appeared incomparably grand. The splendor of that morning I

shall never cease to remember. The atmosphere was so crystalline that light lent to it a peculiar glow. As I looked eastward, the skies had the appearance of sapphire blended with dust of gold; and from the as yet invisible sun a gorgeous fan of radiant beams, of a pale orange color, spread itself over the sky to the zenith. Not a cloud was visible, and this magnificent glory of the Orient steadily grew more and more wonderful for beauty and richness of colored light, when all at once the disk of the bright god of day himself majestically rolled up into sight from behind this towering peak, filling heaven and earth with his dazzling and overpowering light, while the snow clad crests of the mountains caught and reflected his rays with almost undimin[ish]ed brilliancy. The lofty peak beyond the glacier, which added so much to the grandeur of this sublime sunrise is *Mount Milton.** Unfortunately, in taking a view of Milton range from the stony mountain side above mentioned, the peak was hid from view by the clouds. There also we found blue berries in abundance, I never saw anything to excel them. They were dead ripe, very sweet, and the bunches were so large that one would fill a hand cleverly full. Soon after we left this rocky mountain-side we passed Albrede Lake. It is so small that it scarcely deserves the name of lake, especially such a romantic name as *Albreda*. Before we were aware we had passed the watershed of the Thompson, and found a large stream flowing through the mountains from the west and taking its course in an opposite direction from that of the Thompson. This stream Mr. Selwyn afterwards named McLennan River. McLennan had his camp about a mile further down, and he returned early on the 12th and said that they met with an Indian hunter who seems to be well acquainted with this part of the country. He belongs to the Kamloop tribe and lives near there. He and two others were here hunting,

* Plates 56 & 57
* Plates 54 & 55

141

but his two companions were gone to the Jasper House on the east of the Rocky Mountains, while he, his kloo[t]shman and two pappooses were remaining on this side awaiting their return. Mr. Selwyn had met him in his advance trip and engaged him for a short time for the combined parties as a guide through this part of the country. His name is Whooit Pask.[29] Having to remain here a day I took a few views, one of which is 'The Photographer of the Geological Survey in Camp near Albreda Lake.'* The nights are very cold, so much so that last night everything around camp froze up. During this night a fearful gale of wind blew from the south-east, and on the mountains a heavy snow storm raged. At times the roar of the wind among the mountain tops and gorges sounded like distant thunder, only far more dismal. In the morning of the 13th of Oct. the wind continued to blow about as terrifically as it did during the night. On this day we travelled 9½ miles and camped on the banks of Canoe river, 216½ miles from Kamloop and one mile from Cranberry Lake. The trail over which we travelled to-day was very good, leading along low sandy terraces of the mountains. About four miles before we reached Canoe river we crossed a high terrace or rather point of the mountain, extending into the south-east angle of the confluence of McLennan and Canoe rivers. The terrace is about 400 feet high, and the top is level and sandy; about four miles long and two wide, covered with small white pines. After descending we came to Canoe river valley which is three miles wide at this point, and also covered with very small white pine. The whole of McLennan River Valley was burnt at different times, and some of it quite lately. Here, at Canoe River, we met Selwyn and La Rue. They were as far as Tete Juan Cache, but did not see any traces of Mahood or party. The scenery here is very fine. The following morning, for a short time about sunrise, the sky was partially clear and gave us a glimpse of the beauties around us. Turn whichever way we will we have snow clad peaks and ranges of mountains before us. But the grandest are some peaks to the south-east of us, lying between Canoe and McLennan river vallies. These Selwyn called Mount Thompson. East we have Canoe river valley, west Canoe river gap, south McLennan river valley, and north Cranberry lake and Tete Juan Cache Valley, all of which have high mountain ranges on either side, covered with snow, and in many places bold and rugged peaks and bluffs rise high above the general height of the ranges. Immediately across Canoe River (north) rises a high bank or hill about 200 feet in height. A mile beyond this is Cranberry Lake, and a wide valley looking towards Tete Juan Cache and the Fraser River. McLennan, upon hearing that Mahood did not succeed to get through to Cranberry Lake, determined to send his trains back, or such part of them as may stand a chance of getting back to Kamloop. He ordered all his men to return to Kamloop except twelve, consisting of Mr. Green, C.E., in charge, and Mr. Irish, assistant. Having no timber here on Canoe River, either to build huts or for firewood, he had the twelve also to return about 8 miles and make a camp on McLennan River. He and Mr. Selwyn determined to take eight days' provisions, and our best horses, and make a flying visit to Leather Pass and Cowdung Lake[30] in the Rocky Mountains, accompanied by myself, Hammond, La Rue, Philip, and Whooit Pask as our guide. Whooit Pask said that we could easily make the Pass in four days. He gave us to understand that the trail was very good. Upon this decision I got the provisions and photographic instruments ready, although I felt rather averse to this undertaking, and could not enter into it as enthusiastically as some others, the reason being the lateness of

* Plate 58

29 Selwyn calls him 'Jem.' Selwyn, 'Journal and Report,' 41.

30 Present day Yellowhead Lake.

the season, the jaded appearance of the horses, and the almost certainty of being snow-bound on our return to Kamloop.

CHAPTER XI

Flying Expedition to Leather Pass – Cranberry Lake – Tete Juan Cache – Grand Forks of the Fraser – Rough Trail – Moose Lake – The Rocky Mountains – Return to Canoe River Camp

---

The Gazette, July 29, 1872

Early on the morning of the 16th of Oct., we left Canoe river camp, crossed Canoe river, which we forded with ease, (being low at this season of the year), and soon after came to the steep hill, of which I spoke before. This hill proves to be the divide between the waters of Canoe river valley and Cranberry Lake. On the top of it the land is level, sandy, and for some distance covered with young pine, and then we came to a considerable part which had been devastated by fire. About a mile from our camp we got the first glimpse of Cranberry Lake; however, we did not get a good view of it until we went around to the western side. The lake is about three miles long and one wide, and very shallow, so much so that the rushes can be seen scattered all over the lake above the water, making it appear very peculiar. It has also several very pretty little islands, and is covered, at this season of the year, with thousands of wild duck.* Upon the whole the lake is very picturesque. We passed along the western shore, and crossed around the north end, where we found the outlet of the lake – which is very small, only a brook three feet wide and two deep – running through a flat marshy meadow. Soon after passing the northern end

of the lake we came to a beautiful pine grove, and passing through this we came to a large mountain stream of clear water. McLennan named this stream Selwyn river. After fording the river we passed over a very pretty tract of land, and travelling about ten miles when we saw on our left a number of beautiful mountain peaks. As we neared Tete Juan Cache we had to cross sandy benches of the mountain, covered with large juniper-berry trees, or bushes. The mountain scenery also became bolder and more grand. Before us we have the valley of the Fraser, and as far as can be seen, it is hemmed in on each side by high and rugged ranges of mountains. On our right is a large gap in the mountains through which the Fraser River comes rushing and tumbling over a rocky bed, but now not near so large as when we left it at Lytton. Tete Juan Cache is simply a name given to this locality on the Fraser. Nothing is seen here except a place where Tete Juan – a Frenchman, – cached his furs, etc., while hunting, and also an old log hut about ten feet long, eight wide, and only 3 or 4 feet high, all of which are deserted. Here we forded the river and camped. The valley between Canoe river and Tete Juan Cache is about 20 miles long, (the distance we travelled to-day), and 6 miles wide. Much of it is very good land, and quite desirable, if the climate is not too severe in the winter. LaRue is our cook on this 'Flying Expedition,' and it appears that the yeast powders were forgotten, and also the salt. Our supplies on this eight days' trip were, when we started – flour, bacon, sugar, and tea.

At 7.45 a.m., on the 17th of October, we left Tete Juan Cache and started up the Fraser. Soon we came to a very rocky side of a mountain, flattening a little as its base neared the river. The bolders of rock are scattered around thickly in every direction, and in places piled up. It appears as if in some age of the world a great earthquake sundered these mountains of

* Plate 63

rocks into fragments and scattered them as above described. The distance across this rocky ridge is about one-fourth of a mile. We, however, got safely across after a few mishaps, one of which, the *photo.* horse, fell amongst the rocks, and had to be unpacked and raised out of his position, and then repacked. After traveling about four miles we ascended onto a very high bench or terrace of the mountain, from the top of which we saw the first scenes of interest since we left the Cache. The river was about 800 feet below us, and beyond it, is a large mountain with deep gorges and chasms. Soon we descended and came to an open flat by the river. Here our guide left the trail and took to the river and traveled along the shore of, and over small islands in, the Fraser, crossing and recrossing it six or eight times in a distance of about two miles, when we came to the Grand Forks of the Fraser River. Here the view is indescribably grand. Before us rise, as it were, mountains upon mountains of stratified rocks thousands of feet high, the tops of which are covered with perpetual snow, and the gorges filled with glaciers of snow and ice. On our left rises another high mountain rocky and bare. In several places the rocks stand out of the sides of the mountain, bold, jagged, and arched. They look as if in some age there was a fearful upheaval in the earth, – such a shock as it perhaps may never feel again, – and raised the centre of a plain, where these rocks were stratified, and left them in a conical position. The elements wore away one side of them, and thus left the arches of rock exposed to view. Our right is also blocked up with towering mountains covered with the everlasting snows. We were for a moment lost in silent admiration of the charming landscape before us. But time would not permit us to enjoy the scene long; so passing on we followed the north branch of the Fraser for a short distance, and then turned to the right and crossed over a wooded ridge towards the east branch. Altogether we travelled about nine miles on this day, and had the misfortune of losing our tea and sugar on the way, so now we are reduced to flour and bacon, and what few grouse we may shoot on the way, which were very few indeed. On Oct. 18th we did not find all our horses till noon, when we again got on the way, and soon came to a steep mountain bluff extending into the east branch of the Fraser. Here the Fraser is for a considerable distance a continuous rapid. To get beyond this bluff we had to ascend the steep mountain side at an angle of from 37 to 40 degrees, and to a height of about 1,000 feet. After we got cleverly across we passed through thickly fallen timber, which were burnt a number of years since, and now lie prostrate in every conceivable manner, and in going across this we had to turn and twist among, under, and over it in every possible way. The horses had to leap over logs full three feet high, and sometimes two and three at a time. After travelling about five miles we crossed a large ravine, through which runs a brook of considerable size. Ascending the east side we again came to burnt timber along the mountain side, and being 5 o'clock in the evening we camped, and with difficulty got sufficient level ground to pitch our tents, which happened to be in the hollow formed by the uprooting of a tree.

The next day we travelled over the burnt woods; which is about four miles wide, and if anything more encumbered with logs than the trail over which we travelled the day before. After passing over this we again entered the dark forest, and by 1 p.m. we came to a small savanna. Here we lunched and gave our horses an opportunity to graze, which they needed very much, for they had comparatively nothing the past two days. Crossing this prairie we came to a very boggy swamp, yet after a few mishaps we got across all right, and soon arrived at the lower end of Moose Lake,* when

* Plates 60-62

144

we took to the shore and went up the lake about a mile and camped, having travelled only 7 miles. 'A thing of beauty is a joy forever,' and so Moose Lake – although only about ten miles long and four wide – ought to be a joy forever, for veritably it is a thing of beauty. Of all the waters which came to our notice among the mountains this lake is perhaps the most beautiful in itself, as well as the most picturesque in its surroundings. Girdled with a narrow margin of pebbly beach, encircled by dark and stately forests, and overshadowed by towering mountains, from which the glittering snowfields look eternally down into its crystal chambers, this lake wears a charm almost as weird as that which rests over the awe-inspiring canyon of the Fraser. Looking up the lake we see on both sides high and rugged mountain ranges, and far beyond the upper end of the lake the rugged and bold peaks of the Rocky Mountains near the Leather Pass. Turning round we again see mountains and peaks on our right and left, and the front blocked up in the far distance with a beautiful snow-clad mountain. On the 20th of Oct. we were on the way by 7 a.m. This is the fifth day since we left [Canoe] River camp, where our guide – Whooit Pask – told us that we would be at the Pass in four days, and that the trail was good. As is seen from the account of our travels, this trail, with the exception of the first day's travel from Can[o]e river to [T]ete Juan Cache, is anything but good, and we are not at the Pass as yet, but according to the guide's report, we – like Moses – are permitted to look at the coveted spot. Although our flour and bacon was about half consumed, still our desire to reach the Pass and Cowdung Lake was so strong that we put ourselves on half rations, and moved still on. However, before leaving camp this morning we cached three-fourths of the provisions left in order to lighten our packs. This was to supply us on our way back from the lower end of Moose Lake. Well, as I said, by 7 o'clock in the morning we were again on the way, and travelled up the lake along the shore; the greater part of it is very stony and rough, and indeed some places rocky. We passed round the upper end of the lake across a marsh; the grass of which is in many places four or five feet high, but being swamp grass and frosted, the horses, hungry as they were, did not care for it. Some of the swamps were full of ducks, but they were so wild that we could not shoot any. After crossing this marsh we again came to the Fraser, which was lost for the time being in the lake. We followed up this river, crossed numerous small marshes, but soon came to Moose River, which flows through the mountains from the North. After crossing this stream we again entered a low pine forest, and three miles further we crossed another considerable clear water stream also flowing through the mountains from the north, and on our right is another stream flowing through a deep gorge from the South. On this day we travelled about 16 miles, and the greater part of the time it rained.

The next morning still continuing to rain, and being deceived by our Indian guide – Whooit Posk – with regard to the trail, and the distance to Leather Pass and Cowdung Lake – which at the Pass [sic] – and the danger of being snowed in, and also our supplies being exhausted, we all decided that it would be advisable to return; although the guides said that if we went on we could get to Cowdung Lake by evening. The distance from Canoe River to this camp (7 miles above Moose Lake) is about 57 miles. This distance was not paced, so we only give an estimate, and believe it to be as above stated. Thus on the 21st of Oct. we turned back and retraced our steps, took up our cached provisions at the lower end of Moose Lake as we passed, and camped in the small savanna in which we lunched on the 19th.

The next day we made an early start. In crossing the high bluff of which I spoke on the 18th, Dick gave out, although he was led the greater part of the way. We had to abandon him on the highest point of the trail, and it was indeed with a sad heart that I parted with him. We arrived at the Grand Forks of the Fraser at 4 p.m. and camped. The following day we offered our guide a couple of dollars to go back and see what had become of Dick. To our delight the guide brought him back with him, although the poor fellow was too weak to even carry a saddle. While waiting for the Indian I took a few views at the Grand Forks, although the day was cloudy and rained betimes. After this we returned to Tete Juan Cache, and on the way we found the tea and sugar we had lost on going. This was lucky, for we had nothing left but a little flour. Oct. 24th – We left the Cache, and at Selwyn River I took a few more views, while we were lunching on flour baked without salt or yeast, and only quarter enough of that. However, we divided and were thankful that it was not worse. At 4 p.m. we got back to 'Canoe River Camp,' and found the rest of our party all well. Soon after we began to do justice to the bacon and beans, and our usual yeast powder dampers. Now, with regard to our 'Flying Expedition' to the Leather Pass, I might say that photographically speaking, it was a frantic leap after the shadow and losing the substance. My evil forebodings before we started were unfortunately realized. We lost the opportunity of taking views here at Canoe River, which with a few exceptions, are as good as those we saw above, and the best of which I was not able to take on account of rain and continuous travel. By it we lost the strength of our horses, and also opened ourselves to greater liability of being snowed in and froze up in the mountains, and also by it the difficulty of returning to Kemloop across the mountain at Blue River, etc., was greatly increased.

CHAPTER XII

Departure from Canoe River Camp – Q. Party's Mountain Home – Snow – Abandoning the Horses – Drying and Caching Supplies, &c. – Our Canoe Fleet – Departure of the Fleet – McLennan's Trains – Rapids – Canoe Capsized – Murchison's Rapids – Upper Gate – Lower Gate

On the morning of the 26th of Oct. we bid farewell to our camp on Canoe River, and started back for Kamloop. Four months ago on this day, we bid farewell to our friends in Montreal, and now, after working ourselves further and further away from home for four months, on the same day of the month, we begin to retrace our steps. After travelling 8 miles we came to Mr. Green's, and his party's Mountain Home on McLennan River. They had a large cache built of heavy logs about completed, and pretty well stocked with provisions. They had also a large hut in course of erection, which, no doubt, was completed in a short time. I left them some of my 8 x 10 plate glass, to put windows in their mountain house, thus in a short time they will be quite comfortably situated except being isolated from the civilized world. The winter, no doubt, will be very long and dreary for them here – far away in the wilderness. After bidding them adieu we travelled on and camped near Albreda Lake. About midnight it began to snow, and the next morning we had a quilt of about six inches of snow over us, but soon after we shook the snow off us it began to rain and continued for about two hours, when it again began to snow and continued all day. We travelled this day to where we camped, October 7th, and it was very tiresome plodding through the soft snow, which was eight inches deep. It was dark when we began to pitch our tent and being tired and wet, we did not feel in a very good mood. However, after we had our tents up, we made a large camp fire, dried our clothing and boots – the latter as well as the former were about as wet inside as out – and then turned into our blankets, and were soon lost in sleep. Poor Dick had again to be abandoned, and this time for good, as well as one of the pack-horses, which gave out and was left. This evening at supper I suggested to Selwyn and McLennan that I thought it would be far better for us, after we got to the Forks of the North Thompson, to send the remaining horses back to Cranberry Lake to winter, as I thought it would be impossible for them to get back to Kamloop. There may be a possibility to save some of them at the lake. There was considerable grazing at the lake, although not of the best; yet if the winter is not too severe, and snow too deep, and the animals not too weak, they may see the winter through.

On the 28th of October we arrived at the Forks of the North Thompson. Here McLennan's party built a cache of large logs, as they were returning, and in it they had cached about five thousand pounds of flour, and some other supplies. On the following day Mr. Selwyn and McLennan determined to abandon the horses, and send them back to Cranberry Lake by one of Mr. Green's men, who happened to come down with us to the Forks, and build canoes and go down the Thompson; and this we had to do in haste, for we were in great danger of being frozen in. Already there was considerable floating ice in the river, and the weather was rapidly getting colder. We determined that it was necessary for us to have four canoes, two of which were already made, and the Indian Pask agreed to sell the one which was above at the Indian grave (of which I spoke before, and it appears to be the grave of one of his associates). Thus we had but one

canoe to make. Four men engaged at this, and for two days half of the party were engaged in overhauling the floor in the cache, drying blankets, mantles, etc.[31]* We estimated that it would take eight days for our canoe fleet to reach clear water [Clearwater River], and for this time I weighed out the necessary provisions from the cache. Our party now consisted of twelve persons, viz: – Our party of eight, Mr. McLennan, two of his Indians, and the guide, Whooit Pask.

On the night of the 30th about twelve inches of snow fell, so we had the next day eighteen inches of snow. About 10 a.m. the clouds cleared away, and the sun shone bright and warm; and as far as the sky was concerned, it was a pleasant day; but under us, we had eighteen inches of slush; over us, the trees were laden with snow, which melting by the sun, came down in showers of water, and at times the snow came down 'with a run' from the highest part of a tree, and brought all below it along. Through this I walked about six miles to see after the new canoe, and it was rather an interesting journey. The boggy places being covered with snow, I of course could not see them, and frequently, before I was aware, I was down hip deep in mud and slush. Thus upon the whole it was rather *jolly* plodding in the woods, in a mild day, after a heavy snow storm. However, the following day it was colder, and a great deal of snow fell. Since the 12th of Sept. we had but very few pleasant days. Rain, *rain*, RAIN, almost day and night, with but very few excepted days, and now it is snow, *snow*.

Our canoes are finished; our caching is completed and photographed; so that on the 2nd of Nov. we left the cache at the Forks of the North Thompson, and sailed down the river in our fleet of 4 canoes. The largest canoe was the last made, and this we named 'Snow Flake.' The one made at Canoe Camp, Sept. 21st, was named 'Cedar'; the canoe which is built at the

* Plates 64 & 65

31 As Selwyn relates, one of the survey parties had cached 4000 pounds of flour here. However, because the cache had been hastily built many of the bags had become wet and unless they were dried the flour would have spoiled. Part of his party dried and re-bagged the flour while the others built the canoe. Selwyn, 'Journal and Report,' 45.

Forks, Oct. 4th, was named The 'Thompson'; and the one bought from the Indians we called 'Siwash.' The 'Thompson' was manned by Whooit Pask as captain, and McLennan's Indian, George, as assistant, and in this Mr. Selwyn and McLennan embarked with a light cargo. The 'Snow Flake' was officered by Philip, captain, and Peterson, assistant, and in this Hammond and I embarked, taking with us our photo instruments and materials, and also some provisions. The 'Cedar' was manned by McLennan's Indian, Dick, as captain, and Donald, assistant, with provisions for cargo. The 'Siwash' was manned by LaRue as captain, and Dean, assistant, having blankets and some provisions for their cargo. The cargo in the different canoes, consisting of provisions, blankets, tents, photo instruments, etc., weighed about 1,000 pounds. As I said we left the Forks and sailed down the river in the midst of floating snow and ice. The river, at this season of the year, is low in spite of rain and snow, and there are numerous riffles which we had to cross, and frequently the 'Snow Flake' would stick on the stones and the only way to get her across was to jump out into the river and push her over, and then in again and away. It was rather exciting work to run over the rapids and riffles. A little after one p.m. we had to make a portage around some drift wood, of both cargo and canoes. The distance we traveled this day was, as seen by the trail, 18 miles, but by river fully 25 miles. It rained nearly the whole day, so that by evening, when we camped at 5 o'clock, we were cold and thoroughly wet with the rain, the jumping into the river, and the splashing of the paddles, and our feet were like lumps of ice. Upon the whole canoeing in cold, rainy and snowy weather, on rough water, is pretty *rough* work. Early on the 3rd of Nov., after a night of rain and snow, we again sailed and went six miles below 'Wild Goose Camp,' or eight and a half miles below Blue River. A short distance above 'Wild Goose Camp,' near Blue River, we saw one of Mr. McLennan's retreating party's camps. There they abandoned and cached their pack-saddles, apperagoes, horse blankets, etc. From there down to this evening's camp we saw many sad sights. At 'Wild Goose Camp' we found two mules dead. The poor creatures were abandoned, and one died from hunger and cold on the camping ground; the other, no doubt, went in search of food in a swamp close by, and got mired, and had not strength sufficient to get out. Further down we saw no less than three dead; one in the river, one mired in the sand close to the river, and the other dead among some rocks on the shore. Soon after we saw one poor mule standing on the bank of the river where there was a small bit of grass. When he heard us he looked round at us and brayed piteously, as much as to say, give me help. There he no doubt vainly sought food until weakened by hunger he lay down and died a miserable death. Still further down, and near our camp, we saw a horse lying among the rocks by the bank of the river. Here we had to get out of the canoe to lighten it, in order to run over a pretty bad rapid, and as we passed the horse we saw that he was still alive, but too weak to raise his head; and to get him out of his misery Mr. Selwyn shot him. It was far more pleasant canoeing the second day than the first; the river gradually becoming larger from its numerous tributaries, and therefore the riffles were not so shallow. We, however, passed over a few very angry-looking rapids; in two of them the canoes took in a great deal of water, and had to be bailed out. At our camp this evening there is scarcely any snow. No doubt there was not as much as we had at the Forks and the rains of the past few days melted what there was away. Near here McLennan's retreating party left notice on the bank of the river for us, stating that they were short of provisions. They also say that they sent up the mountain from

'Wild Goose Camp,' and found that it was impossible to cross the mountain on account of the snow, so the only alternative was for them to cut a new trail from Blue to Mad River along the banks of the North Thompson, and get through as best they could.

On the 4th of Nov., after another rainy night, we got on the way by 8 o'clock, but only went about a quarter of a mile when we came to a very large rapid. Here we had to make two portages of our cargo for a distance of a quarter of a mile each, the canoes we let down by ropes. Running, or shooting over the rapids, and making portages was the order of this day, and we only travelled about three miles. Our guide – Whooit Pask – was chief captain and pilot, and he was very cautious, and would not venture much. When there was any danger he had us get out and walk along the shore, while he and LaRue ran the rapid, taking one canoe at a time. Often I found myself offering up a silent prayer, when I saw those two in the frail bark, tossed by the whirling, roaring and foaming water as it rushed over and past huge boulders of rock. Often the water dashed over into the canoe, sometimes four or five gallons at a time, so by evening our cargo, as well as ourselves, was well drenched with rain.

Nov. 5th. – Immediately below the last night's camp is a dangerous rapid. We walked along the shore, and the guide took the lead, alone, in the 'Siwash,' and Philip and LaRue followed in the 'Snow Flake.' They got through, but the 'Siwash' shipped about one-third full of water, and the 'Snow Flake' was half full when she got through and came very near swamping. LaRue and the guide went back and brought the 'Thompson' through; she also took in much water. Again they went back to bring the 'Cedar' down; however, they took all her cargo out except a bundle containing one pair of blankets each for Hammond and me, and my large overcoat; one box with all my 8x10

negatives, and some chemicals; saddle and bridle, three axes, and a bag of beans. All went went well until they got to the lower chute of the rapids; there the canoe capsized, and away went our roll of blankets, etc., skipping over the foaming waters like a feather. Down went the saddle, axes and beans, and *my negatives,* the fruit of a great portion of my labor. One can imagine my feelings about that time, – but wait. The guide left the canoe and swam to the shore, but LaRue stuck to it, and swimming, pushed it as well as he could till we threw him a rope, and pulled him out. After both Indians were safe the canoe was hauled to shore and righted up, when, to our surprise, there was the box containing my negatives, held under the cross-piece of the canoe. This was a strange, and to me a happy occurrence, that everything in the canoe should be lost except the box containing my work, which I valued above everything else. The two Indians were almost frozen before we got a fire made to dry their clothes. After drying my negatives and the Indians' clothing, we passed over another rapid, about a quarter of a mile long, making a portage of the cargo, and camped.

Here the rocks close in on each side, so the river has but a very narrow channel through which it flows.* Immediately below this channel, or rather in the lower end of it, is a large boulder of rock, dividing the water, and on each side of it is a fall of about six feet. The scene both above and below is very fine. The walls of rock on each side are jagged, and appear as if they had been rudely severed asunder in some age, thus leaving a small chasm through which the waters of the North Thompson flow. Hearing that there is another and similar place like this further down, I called this the Upper Gate of Murchison's Rapids. To get below this Gate we had to make a portage of cargo and canoes across the bluffs for a distance of about one-third of a mile, and height about 400 feet.*

We spent the whole of the next day in making the portage, and took the canoes and all the cargo across except what we needed for our camp, which we did not move until the 7th of November, when we at an early hour broke up camp, carried our camp equipments across the Bluff, and again went canoeing. This day we went about one and a half miles, and camped at the upper end of the Lower Gate of Murchison's Rapids. By this it is seen that the distance between the two Gates is only about one and a half miles, certainly not more than two, and the river between them is almost a continuous rapid,* over which we had to let the canoes down with lines. Here at the Lower Gate we had to make a portage of both canoes and cargo for a distance of about one mile, over a bluff which is about 500 feet high, but the top of which is quite level. On the same day we carried our cargo across and camped among the rocks at the mouth of the Lower Gate, and the next day we got the canoes across. The Lower Gate is far the grander of the two, especially viewing it from below.* The rocks for some distance are perpendicular, jagged and ragged, and in many places 200 feet high. The Gate proper cannot be seen from the mouth. In order to get a good view of this we have to cross a bluff several hundred feet high, and descend on to a rock 100 feet above the water. At the narrowest part of the Gate the rocks are not more than 10 feet apart, and through this small opening the large waters of the Thompson forces its way.

Immediately at the mouth of the Gate is a very large eddy, and here we found our roll of blankets floating all right except [for] a complete soaking.

On the 9th of November we travelled about 2½ miles, and again pitched our tents among the rocks. We passed over five large rapids, two of them were half a mile long each. In four of them the boats had to be let down with ropes, and part of the cargo portaged. The past few days we had very pleasant weather, except very cold. The following day we got out of our blankets at four in the morning, — in fact we have been up every morning at 4 and 4:30 since Oct. 16th, when we left Canoe River Camp on our 'Flying Expedition' to Leather Pass, — rolled up our tents, blankets, etc., ate our breakfast, and started at daybreak. Almost immediately we came to a rapid three-fourths of a mile long. Here we let the canoes and cargo down with ropes until we got near the lower end, where we had to make a portage of all our cargo over a low bluff of about 150 yards to get below a small cascade. Below this is a large eddy, and there Murchison's rapids ends, and as is seen, they are a chain of rapids about seven miles long, and the most important points of interest are its two gates.

CHAPTER XIII

Salmon River — Orr's Party — More Rapids — Cascade near the Mouth of Mad River — Snow Storms — Canoe Lost and one Abandoned — Miserable Camp — Photo Instruments and other Materials Abandoned — Walk to Clear Water — Wading Raft River — McLennan's Supply Depot at Clear Water — Another Snow Storm — Whooit Pask's Departure — Camp at Red Pine Indian Reserve — War with the Ice — In Kamloop Again

The Gazette, July 31, 1872

After re-shipping the cargo we again got on the way, and had a pleasant sail the rest of the day over broad, smooth still water. Soon after leaving the last rapids we came to Salmon river

* Plate 68
* Plates 69 & 70
* Plate 71

which flows into the Thompson from the east. It is but a very small stream, and scarcely deserves the name of river. The North Thompson river, from Murchison's rapids, as far as we travelled this day, is very wide and shallow, with sandy banks and numerous shoals. We travelled about twelve miles and camped on the ground where Mr. Orr's party – who were sent out in the summer of 1865 on a prospecting expedition for gold, etc., – built their boats. During the past night it was very cold, and this whole day it has been freezing very hard. The ice was fast forming in the river, and in many places along the banks it is an inch thick.

On the morning of the 11th, after a very, *very* cold night, we found the river full of floating ice, and in calm water had much difficulty in getting through. At daybreak we started, but soon came to rapids again, the running of which was the order of the day. We made one portage of about 400 yards of all of the cargo, and in several places of part.

Selwyn, McLennan and Hammond walked past most of the rapids, but by the request of Philip I remained in the 'Snow Flake,' and helped to paddle across all the bad water except two. It is very exciting indeed to go down some of the rapids. Now we turn to the right to evade a large rock; scarcely are we past this when another is in front of us, and the canoe rushing on at a terrific pace, but by the energetic use of the paddle and steering to the left we escape this; now the canoe goes bumping over some unseen boulder; now we dash into large white caped waves, caused by the water rushing over large boulders of rocks beneath. Now the water splashes into our faces, over us and into the canoe. Soon we reach a small bit of smooth water below and the excitement of the moment is over. It is, however, but for a moment, for soon we enter rapids equally hazardous. Those rapids broke up the floating ice so that below it was nothing but floating slush. This day we travelled about eight miles. Two miles above this evening's camp we passed the flat, from which we turned back to Mad River to cross the mountain, Sept. 1st. On the 12th of Nov., after a stormy night, – during which time considerable snow fell, – we got up at the usual time, and were on the way by eight o'clock. We had a fine run of about four and a half miles when we were brought to a sudden halt by coming to a short but impassable cascade; which is about a quarter of a mile above the mouth of Mad River. In this cascade the water falls about 30 feet in a distance of 100 yards. On each side the rocks rise almost perpendicular to a height of 100 feet. Below the cascade there is a large eddy, this, and a considerable distance below, was blocked up with ice and slush. Here our hardship increased every hour, gradually the thermometer went down to zero, and at noon a heavy snow storm set in and continued all afternoon and evening.

To get around this cascade and blockade of ice below, we had to make a portage of both cargo and canoes, across a bluff 200 feet high. It took us from 10 a.m., till noon, to carry our cargoes to the top of the bluff. Then after eating our lunch of frozen dampers, beef, and bacon, we commenced to haul the canoes up the steep side of the bluff which was at an angle of at least 45 degrees. But Alas! What a sequel! The 'Siwash' we got up all right; next we undertook the 'Cedar,' but after we got her about one-fourth of the way up the rope broke, and away she went down the steep precipice, and over the rocky bank 'with a run,' and launched herself into the centre of the river, and was quickly carried through the cascade, and came out below, bottom up. The last we saw of her was going under the ice blockade.

Next we took the 'Thompson' and attached two ropes to her in order to make her secure. The snow and ice made her very heavy, and it took the united efforts of us twelve to draw her up. The 'Snow Flake' was too heavy so we had to abandon her. Thus we were reduced to two canoes, and 105½ miles from Kamloop. Under these circumstances we determined to load the two canoes as light as possible, and abandon everything else; put two Indians in each canoe to paddle them through, and the rest of us walk.

Thus we put in the canoes what we could, and each took a pack and went to the mouth of Mad River, and camped. This was I think the worst camping we experienced on the whole journey. It was on a small rocky flat, fifteen by twenty-five feet, immediately about the mouth of Mad River. Scarcely any firewood could be got, and then it was late, very cold, and much snow on the ground, and still snowing. Mr. McLennan and Selwyn found a medium place for their tent, but the rest fared poorly. Hammond and I found a place about 2½ feet wide among the rocks, where we lay down in our blankets without camp-fires, and slept as best we could. Thus another Sabbath day's worldly labour was closed with its usual amount of mishaps. The Indians even taught us a lesson when we heard them say, 'Wake kloche mamook Sunday' – (no good to work Sunday) – and no doubt we would have done well, even at this crisis, to have regarded the words, 'Remember the Sabbath day to keep it holy.'

The first thing the following morning we returned to the cascade and brought the remainder of our cargo to Mad River, felled a few trees across the river, and carried the cargo over; loaded the two canoes with the necessary supplies, – of which we were getting very short, – and started them off. With the assistance of Hammond and our packer I carried my photographic outfit above high water mark, and cached them as best we could, and then left on foot, plodding through the snow.[32] The day was very cold, and a heavy snow storm raged

until 1 p.m. We travelled about 10 miles, and camped on the bank of the river immediately below our camping ground of Aug. 29th. The snow was about one foot deep, and it was very tiresome plodding through it; however, we had good camping ground in the evening, and after shoveling the snow away we pitched our tents and made large camp fires. The day before some of my toes were frostbitten, and they gave me much trouble in walking, but I was not the only suffering one. The wind blew fearfully during the night, roaring and howling dismally as it passed through the woods and mountain gorges.

At daylight on the 14th we again began to wade through the snow. It drifted a great deal during the night, and in many places it was knee deep. After travelling 13 miles we came to Raft river. This is about 50 yards wide, and at this season of the year quite shallow – only about three feet deep at the fordable place. The water on each side was frozen in some eight or ten feet, and the rest of the stream was full of floating ice. The only way for us to get across was to wade through the water and ice. But before undertaking this *cold bath* we sat down in the snow on the bank of the river and ate lunch of what little we had, and washed it down with *ice* water, and then broke the ice, and waded through the river to the other side. On we travelled with our wet feet and clothing, and now faster than ever in order to keep us warm, and about sunset we arrived at clear water. The canoes had arrived but a few minutes before. Twice they were ice-bound, and had to make short portages. Here McLennan has one of his men – Mr. Glassy – stationed to take charge of his supplies as they were sent by boat from Kamloop. We were all well tired out, having travelled 20 miles. Glassy prepared for us a good meal, which we all enjoyed largely, for we were on short allowance for some time, having been thirteen days on the way from the

32 The photographic outfit, valued at a little more than six hundred dollars by Notman, was recovered in the Spring of 1872 and at least part of it was apparently sold to Richard Maynard, a Victoria photographer.
PAC RG 45, vol. 76, A.R.C. Selwyn to Sandford Fleming, Feb. 24, 1872; Selwyn to George Watt, Feb. 28, 1872; James Richardson to R. Maynard, Feb. 22, 1873; G.R. Grant to R. Maynard, April 15, 1873.

Forks instead of eight as we had estimated.

Here at Clear Water there was only a few inches of snow. Glassy says that the first snow fell on the 12th instant, and that during the summer they had only three days rain up to the time that the snow fell on the 12th of November. What a contrast to the rain and snow we had above Blue river.

McLennan has a large amount of supplies here in charge of Mr. Glassy, who is to forward them up the Thompson river in the spring. Fortunately for us, Mr. McLennan had a flat-bottom boat here, used by Mr. Glassy as a ferry boat. The following day – Nov. 15th – we took this boat, two canoes, and fresh supplies, and rowed down the river amidst thickly floating ice. Soon we passed the mouth of Clear Water, which is free from ice – its waters flowing from lakes, hence warmer, and thus causing the ice in the North Thompson to disappear in a short distance below Clear Water. We had no sooner left camp and passed the mouth of Clear Water, when a terrific snow storm set in, and continued for two hours. At times we had fears for the safety of our canoes. The trees were falling on each side of the river, and sounded much like the distant thunder of a cannonade. However, in two hours the storm ceased, yet continued snowing until 2 p.m.

After travelling eight miles, we came to the old crossing. Here we overtook McLennan's Spanish packers with the remains of their mule train, only eleven, poor, miserable-looking creatures, some of which, I thought, would never reach Kamloop. Here, also, were a few Indian hunters with their families temporarily encamped. Whooit Pask, the Indian guide, knew them and stopped with them to return to the 'Mountain Home' of Mr. Green and party, on McLennan River. We engaged a few of these Indians to go up to Mad River and bring our photographic instruments, chemicals, etc., and cached them down to Kamloop. After making all necessary arrangements, and leaving messages for Mr. Green, we bid Whooit Pask farewell, and again betook ourselves to our boat and canoes. At 2.30 p.m. we were 30 miles below Clear Water, at Red Pine Indian Reserve, where we had camped on the 23rd of Aug., on our way up. Fortune's house was now occupied by the Indian chief, and it not being his, he kindly gave us three-fourths of it for our camp. This is the same chief we met on our way up, and he is as talkative and as fond of oratory as ever. Having suffered much with the cold during this day, and experiencing a very cold night, I bought some furs from the chief the next morning, and wrapped them around my feet, put on all the clothing I had, and over this put one of my blankets, and thus kept quite comfortable. Some of the others, who did not take the same precaution this morning – Nov. 16th – suffered very much with cold.

At 8:30 a.m., we bid *Klahowya* to the *Tyee* (chief), and rowed without anything of interest, thirty-one miles, and at dark arrived at Knouff's ranch. Here we overtook Mr. Cooney, another of McLennan's packers, and also a number of his men who are on their way back. Knouff kindly granted us the privilege of sleeping on 'the soft side of the floor' of his house, and also the use of his fire to fry our bacon.

At day-break the next morning we were again in our boat and canoes, paddling and rowing down stream. But in a few minutes we came to a sudden halt, the river being blocked up with ice for some distance, around which we had to make a portage. This detained us about two hours. Here Philip, in crossing on the ice, broke through, but fortunately caught himself by the edge of the ice and held on till a rope was thrown to him, and thus was saved from a watery grave. We had a regular race, and war with the ice the whole remaining distance to Kamloop. At one place, three miles from Kamloop, we came very near being jammed up between two large fields or cakes of ice, but with hard work and pushing we finally got through and arrived at Kamloop, and thus bid farewell to the *North Thompson* river. We all with happy hearts exclaimed '*In Kamloop again, nearing the civilized world,* for which we feel grateful to God.'

CHAPTER XIV

Reminiscences of the Expedition up the North Thompson River Valley to Leather Pass

---

The Gazette, August 1, 1872

The day after we arrived at Kamloop the weather was much milder than what it had been the previous two or three weeks. Now since we are back, and will remain in Kamloop for a few days, I might say a word or two further with regard to our trip up the North Thompson, and the utility of this valley as a railroad. As I before stated, McLennan's party left Kamloop with about one hundred and thirty-five animals, consisting of pack and riding horses, and mules. Our party had 15 horses, making in both parties 150 animals. These as seen before were worn out by labor, and weakened for want of proper nourishment, so that out of the above number only 26 got back to Kamloop. What of the rest? Many died on the way; some were abandoned, because too weak to travel further, the fate of those, no doubt, is death by starvation and exposure, and a number were left at Cranberry Lake with the hope that they may winter through. But why were they left? Evidently because they were too weak to make the journey to Kamloop, and therefore, I fear too weak to brave the long winter among the mountains

at Cranberry Lake. (Since writing the above I received a letter from Mr. McLennan's Assistant Commissary, in which he states that all the horses and mules left at Cranberry Lake are dead.) The agricultural and mineral prospects of the North Thompson River Valley are very limited, there being but very very little farming land to be found. From Kamloop to Clear Water the mountains on either side rise higher and higher, and gradually become more thickly timbered. From Clear Water to Canoe river it can best be described by saying that the North Thompson is a large stream of water running between two high ranges of mountains very heavily timbered with giant cedars, hemlock, pine, balsam and poplar or cotton wood trees, with an undergrowth of hazel, tall cranberry and other bushes, and the ever detestable Aralea.

As to the minerals I believe there are but few to be found; but with regard to the Geological interest of the valley, I refer the reader to Mr. Selwyn's able report. Yet, notwithstanding this unfavorable description of the North Thompson River Valley, it has an important redeeming feature. It is perhaps the easiest and best gap for the Canadian Pacific Railroad to pass through the Rocky Mountains. The grade is very gentle; the highest point – which is at Leather Pass – being only about 4,500 feet above sea level. The only difficulty which may stand in the way are the heavy snows of the long winters.

No route on the continent could boast of scenery as rugged, grand and awe-inspiring as would be seen by the Western-bound traveller as he nears the Rocky Mountains, and rushes past peaks, columns, domes, glaciers, lakes, cascades, over sparkling streams, and through stately forests of the giant cedar, fir and hemlock trees. His heart would be continually thrilled with delight and awe, as he would gaze upon this charming panorama. There is

Mount Brown rising to the enormous height of 16,000 feet. At its base the cars would thunder along, while its peak extends far above the clouds; or should the sun lend its radiant light, the mountain crest ever covered with snow would reflect the light of the ruler of the day, and thus make the opening scene a masterpiece of this panorama of Nature.

Rushing on he enters Leather Pass. Here walls of rock, mountains of walls, on either hand rise majestically thousands of feet above where snow and ice rule supreme. Now the cars pass Cowdung [Lake, i.e. Yelllowhead Lake] – which is at the highest point of the Pass; – now they rush over crystal streams; now through dark forests; anon they break forth into light and beauty and before him is Moose Lake. Here look where he will, he will behold mountains; mountains bare and bleak; mountains rugged; mountain peaks; mountains clad with perpetual snow; mountains of rock; mountains over whose brow crystal streams of water flow; mountains thickly timbered, at whose base calmly repose the cold, placid waters of Moose Lake. Hastening on, he soon arives at the Grand Forks of the Fraser. The heart of the tourist must indeed be hard if it is not touched with the scenes now before him. It will stir within him feelings which he cannot express, nor are words able to paint the scene. Stopping but a moment to note the beauties around him, the cars whirl him through a narrow mountain gorge with the turbulent waters of the Fraser at his feet, until he arrives at Tete Juan Cache. Here, again, his heart and eyes will be delighted with new scenes, and in response he can only exclaim: How grand! how sublime! But no time for reverie, for the iron horse gives the signal and away the long train speeds through Tete Juan Cache Valley in continual sight of snow-clad mountains; past Cranberry Lake, bestudded with islands, and teeming with wild duck; on, across Canoe

River and Valley; past the rugged peaks of Mount Thompson, and in a few moments the tourist is in full view of Mount [Milton].

If the orb of day should now [rise in the] Orient, the tourist would be rich[ly rewarded] for having travelled many hundred [miles], if only to behold this one scene of transcendent beauty, whose charms have already been described in a previous chapter.[33]

But the cars speed him on past Albrede lake; past the forks of the North Thompson, and now they enter the dark forests, still in their primeval glory. As he rushes on through these mighty old forests, he gets a glimpse of Garnet River Cascade, Mount Cheadle, and numerous other cascades, rugged peaks and glaciers equally grand. Arriving at Blue River Station it would be well for him to stop for several days to behold some of the charming scenes of the Selkirk range of mountains, and Selwyn lake, the beauty of which has already been described in the 7th chapter. Ascending the mountain he would be greeted by a beautiful lakelet at the summit; but this has no charms when compared with the sublime scenes which open out before him. The wearisome journey up the mountain would soon be forgotten as he now sits and gazes upon glaciers and snow-clad ranges of mountains on every hand; the dark valley of the Thompson 4,000 feet below; and lake Selwyn far off to the West. He would be so enraptured and lost in wonder and awe that he would not perceive that the day was rapidly fading away until he beheld the sun sinking behind the western cliffs. Having other scenes of beauty and grandeur to visit, he descends by the moon's pale light, and the next day winds his way up Blue river to Selwyn lake. After spending a few days pleasantly in sailing over its placid waters, and beholding the delightful scenery which ever and anon greet[s] the eye, he returns and again enters the cars which whirl past the torrents of Murchison's Rapids

33 Newspaper torn.

and its twin Gates; on past bluffs, over crystalline streams, over small savanas and prairies, till finally he reaches the silvery waters of Kamloop Lake, when he is fairly through the Rocky Mountains and North Thompson Valley. But there are other scenes of grandeur and sublimity in store for him as the cars whirl him past this lake, down the Thompson; across, past, and through sandy hills covered sparsely with sage brush and bunch grass; down the Fraser Canyon, along its bluffs and walls of rock, with the angry torrents of the Fraser hundreds of feet below, battling with every element which may come in its way to retard its progress; till suddenly he emerges forth to light, and he is at the little village of Yale, which guards the entrance of the canyon.

The grand and majestic scenery of the Trans-Continental Railroad from Omaha to San Francisco would almost sink into oblivion when compared with the sublime and awe-inspiring panoramic scenes which ever and anon greet the eye as the cars would rush through the Rocky's; down the North Thompson Valley, and through the cascades. Thus this valley may yet become renowned as a place of grandeur and beauty to the tourist, if not for mineral and agricultural productions.

CHAPTER XV

Departure from Kamloop – Mr. Fortune's Farm on Spallumcheen River – Journey to Bonaparte – Waggon Ride to Yale – Canoing to New Westminster – Sail to Victoria – Mr James Richardson – Voyage to San Francisco – Ten Days in the Cars from the Pacific to Montreal – Photographs of British Columbia

---

On the 20th of November, we hired a small

boat, and at 1 p.m. bid farewell to Kamloop, and having a good wind, we sailed down through Kamloop Lake to Savona Ferry by 7.30 o'clock in the evening. Here we met Alexander Fortune, who has a large farm of 600 acres on Spallumcheen River, B.C. This river empties into Shooshap Lake. He says that his farm needs no irrigation, and that he is able to raise from forty to fifty bushels of wheat per acre.

The next morning we tried to get a team to go to Bonaparte or Cash Creek, but Mr. Urin, the landlord of the Savona Inn, had all his horses on the mountains grazing for the winter. However, he sent an Indian to try to find them. At 4 p.m. the Indian returned, and brought several horses, but only one was fit to be put into a wagon. So Selwyn concluded to get riding horses, and one pack horse. It rained nearly the whole day, and at 8.30 in the evening we left Savona Ferry on horseback in a drenching rain, and travelled all night, arriving at Bonaparte the next morning at 5 o'clock. It rained all night, and, as can be expected, we had a miserable night of it. We had expected to meet the stage in the morning at Bonaparte, but it did not arrive until evening, and it was then already overcrowded, so there was no chance for us in that direction.

After much difficulty we got a waggon, and left Bonaparte at 11 a.m. of the 23rd of November, and arrived at Cook's Ferry at 8 o'clock in the evening. The roads were very bad, and at every hill we had to walk up. The following day we travelled to Lytton. As I said before, Lytton is a stormy place, and in the evening the wind blew a perfect gale, snowing a little and freezing hard.

During the forenoon of the 25th a terrific snow-storm raged. The ground was froze quite hard, so that travelling in the wagon, *minus springs,* was very rough work. At 8 a.m. we left Lytton and drove over the rough road, and through the snow-storm, until we got to Boston Bar, at 6 p.m. The thermometer read zero in the morning, at noon rose to 10 degrees above zero, but in the evening fell again to zero.

The next day we left Boston Bar at 8 a.m., and arrived at Yale at 5 p.m. Three miles from Boston Bar we came to Chinaman's Bluff. Part of the bridge at the top spanning the gorge was carried away by a slide of rock from the bluff above. We managed, however, to get across by running the waggon across a few poles tied together, and leading the horses across one at a time. The day was very cold, and more or less snow fell. We were still not out of all difficulties. We expected to find a steamer here, but the river was so full of floating ice that she could not get up, and the telegraph lines were down in every direction, so no news could be received of the boat. The following day at noon we embarked in a canoe, hired to carry the mail and express, and paddled amid floating ice as far as Hope.

On the 28th of November we left Hope half an hour before daylight, and sailed to New Westminster by 10.30 p.m., distance 85 miles. We had much floating ice to contend with until we passed Schomez, which is some distance below the mouth of Harrison's river. At the latter river we saw the steamer *Hope* ice bound. She made an attempt to get to Yale, but could go no further. This caused much suffering and inconvenience at Yale. Many persons were there from Cariboo and other places desiring to return to Victoria, and others had large numbers of bullocks, which they wished to bring down, as there was but very little hay or straw at Yale, and what little they had sold from four to six cents per pound. Many of the bullocks were already dying from hunger and exposure. We heard that hundreds of animals perished further north, and at Peace river. At New Westminster we were glad to find the steamer *Enterprise* moored and ready to sail to

Victoria early next day. The thermometer averaged this day 22 degrees. In the evening it began to snow and continued all night. Early the next morning we sailed in the *Enterprise* for Victoria, arriving there at 4.30 p.m. No snow at Victoria, and I was told that they had none up to this time. Our friends greeted us with a hearty welcome, foremost of which was Mr. Richardson, geologist.

From him I learned that after he left us at Kamloop, on the 17th of Aug., he explored a portion of the coasts of Kamloop Lake, then returned to Bonaparte, took a stage and went to Cariboo, and returning, explored the country along the Yale and Cariboo road as far as Yale. Then he sailed to Victoria and began his labours along the coasts of Vancouver's Island. He found and collected a large number of very interesting specimens of minerals, etc., and also coal fields, one of which is large, sufficient to supply the North-west coast many years hence. The work he had in view was not completed, so he did not return with us to Montreal, but remained till the next steamer.

Among other pleasantries which we enjoyed after our arrival at Victoria, was the reception of letters from home. This was the first Hammond and I received from our friends since we left home, which was now five months.

After spending eight days in Victoria – (the whole of which time it rained day and night, more or less, except two days) – we sailed in the steamer Prince Albert for San Francisco on the morning of the 8th of Dec., and after a long and tedious voyage we arrived at this place at 2.30 a.m. of the 15th of Dec. Instead of being only from three to four days in sailing from Victoria to this 'Sunset City of the Sea,' we were out just one week.

On the morning of the 10th of December the engine of the steamer broke down, and thus she, for a few days, was scarcely more than able to hold her own against the head wind. Fortunately the wind changed on the 13th, when all the sails were hoisted. This and the little propelling power left in the engine brought us to our desired haven on the 15th.

At 8.30 of the following morning we left San Francisco and sailed up San Francisco Bay, – in the beautiful steamer Capital, – to Vallejo, distance 28 miles. Immediately after, we took a sleeping car and started on the California Pacific Railroad for Sacramento. The country along this railroad to the above city is undulating and almost entirely destitute of trees, and what few do grow are the low scrub oak. The soil, however, appears to be very good, and many, very many, beautiful farms are to be seen. The climate at this season is delightful, the thermometer ranging from 58 to 65 degrees. At Sacramento the gardens look green, and the cabbage was in every stage of growth. All the way from Vallejo to Auburn the farmers were busily engaged in plowing and sowing. At Auburn we gradually began to ascend the western slope of the Sierra Nevada mountains, and at 9.30 p.m. we arrived at the summit of the Sierra. Here the thermometer stood at 30°, and a great deal of snow was seen.

The next day, Dec. 17th, we breakfasted at Humbolt; thermometer 14° and no snow, dined at Battle Mount, and took supper at Elko.

The following morning we arrived at Ogden; the thermometer here read 42°. Here we were delayed till the afternoon, when we again got on way, now on the Union Pacific. As we ascended the Wasatch and Echo Canyon, the wind blew a strong gale, and the snow, which was about six inches deep, drifted rapidly. The train however, made good time until the morning of Dec. 19th, when we began to be detained from one cause or another at the different stations. At Rawlins we got an extra engine to our train. As we neared Percy the train ran through a snow drift; no damage

however, was done, except to the cowcatcher of the front engine, which was repaired after a few hours delay. Half way between Carbon and Medicine Bow the train again ran into a large snow drift or bank. This time the front engine was almost completely wrecked, its tender being piled up onto the front of the back engine, breaking its cowcatcher and the front works of the engine. The snow was from 4 to 5 feet deep. This accident occurred at 6 p.m. [T]he conductor walked to Medicine Bow, and got a wreck train to come to his relief. By the next morning they had the tender on its trucks and the front baggage car on the track. After a tedious delay we again got on the way at 4 p.m., of the 20th. Near Lookout there were five engines blocked with the snow, and off the track, one of these we saw lying beside the track a complete wreck.

At 8 o'clock the next morning we breakfasted at Sidney. We found nothing on the table, and the waiters were so very slow in providing that before we were half done the train started off without giving the usual signal, and thus left Mr. Selwyn, me, and a great number of others behind. Fortunately there was another express train immediately behind. In this we caught up with our train at 3 p.m., at North Platte. At or near Lodge Pole we passed a very large herd of antelope, about 1,500 or 2,000 in number. This morning it was much colder, and as we moved eastward the thermometer gradually fell, and read as following:

At Sidney, 8 a.m., 28°; Plum Creek, 6 p.m., 10°; Kearney, 8 p.m., 7°, and the wind blowing a fearful gale and snowing.

At 9.30 a.m., of the 22nd, we arrived at Omaha. Here we found six or seven inches of snow which fell during the night, and the temperature much milder than the evening before at Kearney. At 5 p.m. we left Omaha on the Burlington and Missouri Railroad, and ate supper in a dining saloon car which was attached to the train for four hours. The thermometer averaged about 20° during the day.

About 4.30 p.m. a terrific snow storm set in, which lasted till the next day at noon. This detained the train about five hours during the night. Although there were two engines to the train, yet they were not able to plow their way through the snow, and draw the heavily-laden train after them. The snow was fully a foot deep where we were at 7 a.m. of the 23rd. Our train was unusually heavy, having three train-loads across the U.P.R.R. on board. After the road was beaten by the engines we again got under way, and at 12.39 p.m. arrived at Mount Pleasant, Iowa. This is a beautiful place in every respect. The storm has passed over, and the sun is shining pleasantly. At Burlington they had scarcely any storm, only a little rain and sleet during the night. As we neared Chicago the snow gradually became less, until it entirely disappeared at the above place.

We arrived at Chicago at 12 a.m. on Sunday morning, Dec. 24th. After breakfast I wandered over the burnt district of Chicago[34] and saw many sad sights of the ruins of this once grand, great and prosperous city of the West. Here are the remains of Chicago's ancient glory. Desolation rules supreme. But enough has already been said of this sad conflagration, and what I might say would only be a repetition of the old story: I therefore will keep silent.

At 5.15 p.m. we left Chicago by the Michigan Central R.R., on our homeward journey. At 3.30 the next morning we arrived at Detroit, and a few hours after we entered the cars of the Grand Trunk R.R., and travelled without much to interest us till we reached Montreal at 1 p.m. of the 26th of Dec. Thus after being absent exactly six months, (having left on the 26th of June and returning home on the 26th of December) during which time we travelled nearly 10,000 miles by cars, ocean and river steamers, stages, sailing vessels, canoes, on rafts, horse back, and on foot, we ended our chequered expedition. As is seen, the first part of the journey was most delightful, but the last part was the extreme of *delightless,* except what pleasure we could get in *'roughing it,'* which was not a little.

Messrs. Selwyn and Richardson will, no doubt, in a short time give valuable reports, showing the mineral resources of this part of British Columbia, which was explored by them.

Photographically speaking, our trip was not as successful as I had anticipated. The season being so late, the difficulty of travel among the mountains so great; the continuous rains, and winter setting in so early, did much to retard our success. Yet I took a goodly number of 8 x 10, and stereo negatives of both geological and general interest. These I was successful in bringing home, although we had to abandon our photographic instruments in the mountains.

All who are interested in British Columbia and our travels would no doubt be further interested and benefitted by these photographs, copies of which can be had from Mr. Wm. Notman, Photographer to the Queen, at his Studio in Montreal. The photographs are interesting, novel and peculiar, and should elicit an inspection.

34 This fire is traditionally blamed on Mrs. O'Leary's cow. It began October 8, 1871 and levelled Chicago.

This book has been printed in an edition of 2000 copies,
Fall 1978, by The Coach House Press, Toronto.
The papers are Warrens Lustro Offset Enamel and Rolland Zephyr book laid.
The type is Baskerville with display in Thorne Shaded.
The plates are micrograin duotone photo offset reproductions from the original
photographic prints.
Published with the kind assistance of the Canada Council and the Ontario Arts Council.